Praise for *First th*
Then the Ice Cream

"If you think that reading this book will magically lead to the perfect child, you will be disappointed. But get this book if you're interested in learning how to raise your child or adolescent in our complex world. You will find clear, common sense recommendations supplied alongside real world examples.

"Parenting is hard work, but armed with these research-supported techniques, you will be better prepared to tackle the enormous task of being a mom or dad."

—**Susan M. Wilczynski, Ph.D., BCBA**

"Psychologist Tim Riley has written an ideal parenting book on discipline. In fact, his advice transcends his own subject and could easily serve as an entire parenting philosophy. Likening discipline to gravity, a fact of life that gives no warnings, explanations, or second chances, he stresses the importance of consistency and repetition as the foundation for emotional stability in children. Emphasizing that rules without consequences are just suggestions and reminding us that anything over seven-words is a lecture, he has an understated and humorous approach that is personal and effective. Riley's style is warm and engaging, and he clearly cares for children and their well-being. Riley's solid contribution is highly recommended."

—★ *Library Journal* **starred review**

"With clarity, wit and wisdom, Dr. Tim Riley, offers a key understanding of why children do what they do as he skillfully guides moms and dads in developing their own structured approach to effective discipline. Parents will appreciate the friendly tone, real life examples and sensible, specific strategies for a variety of common challenging behaviors."

—**Gail Reichlin,**
Executive Director of The Parents Resource Network
and co-author of *The Pocket Parent*

"*First the Broccoli, Then the Ice Cream* is essentially a how-to manual for parents to get their children to do what they are supposed to do, regardless of the situation. Riley holds a doctorate in psychology and is a psychologist and a former professor of pediatrics at the University of Nebraska Medical Center. His private practice focuses on families and children, and his expertise includes treating ADD/ADHD, anxiety and other emotional and behavioral issues.

"Riley also helps families set achievable tasks for their children. The strategies offered in the book are simple to follow and include tips on how to modify the strategy if it isn't working for your child. Parents, caregivers, and teachers will benefit from the behavioral strategies offered here."

—★ ★ ★ ★ ★
ForeWord Clarion Review

"If you have kids, plan to someday, or just want to know how they work, check out my dad's new book. It has my whole-hearted, admittedly nepotistic, endorsement."

—**Andrew Riley, M.A.**

FIRST
THE
Broccoli
THEN
THE
Ice Cream

A PARENT'S GUIDE
TO DELIBERATE DISCIPLINE

FIRST ᴛʜᴇ Broccoli THEN ᴛʜᴇ Ice Cream

A PARENT'S GUIDE
TO DELIBERATE DISCIPLINE

DR. TIM RILEY

TWO FISH BOOKS
Omaha, Nebraska

ISBN10: 0-9841423-1-2
ISBN13: 978-0-9841423-1-6
Library of Congress Control Number: 2009934979
Cataloging in Publication Data on file with publisher.

Two Fish, Books
PO Box 540094
Omaha, NE 68154
www.TwoFishBooks.com

Cover Design: Sammy Gross, 144 Design
Production, Distribution, and Marketing:
    Concierge Marketing Inc.

Printed in the United States of America
10 9 8 7 6 5 4 3 2 1

To Glen and Lillian, Richard and Florence

Contents

Introduction

E than was seven or eight when he came into my office, a tousle-haired, bright-eyed, very active, and completely charming little boy. "I think he might have ADHD," his mother told me. She was obviously very concerned and more than a little upset.

Apparently, some well-intentioned individual with not quite enough knowledge about behavioral health had suggested that Ethan "looked like" a child with Attention Deficit Hyperactivity Disorder. As nearly as I could tell, the main reasons for concern seemed to be that Ethan didn't listen very well, was hard to get to bed most nights, and seemed to "get really mad about almost anything."

After asking a few more questions, having a good look at Ethan, and talking with him for a while, I suggested it was unlikely that he had ADHD and that there was a good chance we could get some improvement in his mood and behavior. It turned out that Ethan and his family were struggling with some very common pressures of modern life. His problem behavior was not the result of some deep-seated problem or psychological disorder, but simply an understandable reaction to what was going on in his world.

Just like in a lot of other families, Ethan's parents were busy trying to take care of work, a home, a checkbook, car, school, cooking, shopping, laundry, and, oh, by the way, managing the behavior of an energetic little boy and his brother and sister. Schedules and routines changed every day as they tried to keep up with all of their own obligations and also tried to get Ethan and his siblings to baseball, gymnastics, piano lessons, Tae-Kwon-Do, play practice, (take a deep breath), swimming, and tutoring. His parents had few chances to communicate as they passed each other on the way to one event or another.

It was hard to sort out Ethan's bedtime issues because there were so many different bed times to choose from. Bedtime might be anywhere from 8:00 to 11:00 or later depending on what was going on for the family that night and when they got home, fed themselves, and actually were ready for bed. He sometimes had a hard time getting to sleep because his body was telling him he should stay up as late as he did the night before or he was so wound up from the activities of the evening that he just couldn't settle.

Ethan did tend to get upset often, though this seemed to be more out of frustration than anger. Ethan was having a hard time figuring out what he was supposed to be doing and when because routines and expectations changed so often. When he did get mad or upset, he noticed that people would pay attention to him and sometimes give him what he wanted to get him to calm down.

Acting angry worked well for him, so he kept doing it. Soon enough, his parents learned to "tiptoe around him" and try to give him what he wanted even before he started to complain. It was just easier. Even the possibility that he *might* get upset got him more of what he wanted. His parents felt trapped and out of ideas.

After three or four sessions with me, things did get a lot better for Ethan and his family. Those sessions were spent mainly just discussing and implementing the ideas and methods in this book. We worked together to create an environment that made more sense to Ethan's little brain.

With some guidance, some practice in my office, and a bit of effort, his parents helped Ethan to learn that he could get most of what he wanted when he was behaving well and that he would be ignored or punished when he was not. They learned to respond to him (and his siblings) the same way from one day to the next, one behavior to the next, and no matter which parent was involved. They learned not to get too wrapped up emotionally in dealing with typical little kid behavior.

We actually did talk about a specific method for improving Ethan's behavior at bedtime (the same one mentioned later in this book), but never had to use it. After a while, Ethan got used to following his parents' instructions during the day and just kept going right into the night, all the way to bedtime. More importantly, his mood stabilized and improved too. As his world became more predictable and made more sense to him, he felt more comfortable and secure.

It doesn't always go exactly this way, of course, but all of the therapists in my office have seen this kind of big change in kids whose parents thought they were completely unreachable. I wrote this book because these are the topics my colleagues and I talk about with parents, week after week, year after year. These are the issues that almost every family deals with at some point.

For many of these families, a few new strategies and a little more focused effort are all that is needed to produce big improvements in their household and their children. We work together to make a few simple (but often not easy) changes in how they structure things in their home and how they approach discipline and motivation. These are the fundamental elements of Deliberate Discipline. They form the core of this book and the foundation for successful parenting, even when there are other, more serious issues to be dealt with.

A casual approach to parenting is not likely to succeed. Every day, your children face constant and intense competition for their attention and loyalty from a thousand different directions, many of them not at all helpful. If you hope they will somehow automatically pick up only *your* values, ideas, and behaviors, there is a good chance you will be disappointed. If you want to be heard above all the noise and stimulation in your children's lives, you must act deliberately and persistently, with a purpose and a plan.

Most of the parents I work with are more than willing and eager to help their kids learn to behave better; they just don't know how. Somewhere along the line, these ideas and methods got blurred or lost in a cloud of well-meaning misinformation.

THE BAD NEWS

A lot has changed about our world and our culture, and many of these changes complicate our children's lives and our own and make the job of parenting a lot more difficult. There was a time when we could count on most adults to have similar expectations for child behavior. Children had a good idea about how they were supposed to act because the rules were basically the same at school and at home and also at most of the houses up and down the block.

Most parents made it clear to their kids that they were expected to listen to adults and follow basic social rules all the time. Kids were reminded often about the value of manners and personal responsibility and held accountable when they missed the mark.

Those days are gone. Rude and coarse behaviors are tolerated by some without comment or correction. Countless television programs present adults (especially parents) as stupid or incompetent. Worse still, some parents seem to have almost no expectations for their kids' behavior, at home or in public, and many parents are ready to do battle with teachers or anyone else who might have the nerve to try to hold their kids accountable. Some parents tolerate (or, worse yet, participate in) disrespect toward other adults, then are surprised and upset when their children do not treat *them* with respect.

It also was not so long ago that a child looking for something to do might be able to choose from among a ball, a bike, two or three channels of crummy television shows, a doll or two (or a few plastic "army guys"), and not much else. Those times have disappeared in a blizzard of technology. Kids still ride bikes of course, but now they also have motorized cars and scooters, *dozens* of channels of crummy television programs, multiple video game systems, computers, cell phones, action figures, CD players, DVD players, MP3 players, and probably some other kind of player invented in the time it took me to write this sentence.

Some kids have so much stuff, in fact, that their parents tell me they have a toy room in their homes just to hold all the stuff that has overflowed their children's bedrooms and closets. For many of these children, though, the only toys they really seem to get excited about are the ones they don't have yet. The children who have the most seem to have the hardest time entertaining themselves and to be the first to complain about being bored. They know how to operate a dozen different gadgets and the names of a hundred video game characters, but can't seem to figure out how to have fun unless it is scripted for them or they are "plugged in" to some electronic device.

As a result of these changes, and many others, life is tougher for kids in a lot of ways. I see the results of these social pressures in my office every day. Many children I meet have come to believe that things are more important than relationships and that everything has a price, but nothing has much value. They seem to have a hard time being satisfied with what they have and always are looking for the next gadget or outfit that will buy them a little status with their peers for a time.

Worse, they believe they are somehow entitled to the mountains of toys and gadgets that fill their bedrooms, closets and toy rooms. They expect that good things should happen for them with little or no effort on their part. They dress and talk like little adults, but are uncertain and insecure underneath.

When everything doesn't come easily or go as expected, they become excessively frustrated, emotionally reactive and lack the persistence to work toward a goal over time.

THE GOOD NEWS

The good news is that some things have not changed. The way kids learn and the basic principles of behavior have not changed. Most kids are still eager to impress and please adults. They want to grow and learn and feel as if they can accomplish important tasks on their own. They want to be able to make sense of the world around them and to feel loved, safe and secure. And, in spite of all that has changed for the worse, parents and other grown-ups still have it within their power to help their kids reach these goals, to guide them on their way to adulthood ready to face all the joys and challenges they will find there. That is what this book is about.

This book looks at how children learn and the best ways to motivate and encourage them. It is about *how* to teach your kids. What you teach them is up to you. This book is about using science and research and my own experiences with thousands of children to build an understanding of the best ways to approach teaching and training them, day in and day out. It is about understanding and accepting your role as one of the most important people in the world (to your children anyway) and using this authority to help them learn the skills they will need to succeed as adults. It is about developing a plan for parenting, putting the plan into action and keeping it going, even long after you have forgotten most of what is in this book.

Mostly what I hope you will find here are a lot of common sense, practical explanations and real world examples that will illustrate some of the things we know about kids and what you can do to improve their behavior and their lives. I hope you will discover new ways to look at and think about kids and gain a greater understanding of why they do what they do.

What this book is *not* about is making life easier for adults. Sorry. The focus here is on making things better for children, not their parents. It turns out, though, that if you are successful at putting the principles and methods in this book into practice, your life probably will get better. It will get better because your children's behavior will improve and their lives will get better. Children who live in predictable, reliable and structured homes tend to be more emotionally balanced and stable. Children who can follow instructions, accept responsibility and cooperate with others are more pleasant to be around. They get along better with other children and adults. They accomplish more and feel better about themselves in the process.

So, understanding the ideas and using the tools in this book should make day-to-day life better for your kids and for the whole family, but not without some effort. The ideas and techniques in this book are mostly simple, but often not easy. Just like anything of value, they require time, effort and energy. Things will not always go as well or as quickly as you would like. Making a plan for parenting and learning some skills does not guarantee a good outcome, but not taking a deliberate approach just about guarantees a bad outcome.

WHAT'S IN THE BOOK

By the time you finish this book, you should expect to have a good idea of how to work out a structured approach to motivation and discipline and an understanding of how this contributes to the emotional and behavioral health of your children. You will have the tools and procedures you need to make it work. This will not solve all your parenting problems. Sorry again. It does not work that way. There is no one book or plan that can do that. But my experience tells me you will find the ideas and tools in this book truly useful for dealing with what we might call the "symptoms of life." These are the everyday, commonplace issues that come up in every family.

Some of the ideas we discuss may seem fairly obvious, but a lot of parents end up in an office like mine because they are just not sure how to handle these day-to-day issues or they lack confidence in their skills or the conviction to follow through. So, even though this book will not address all of your parenting concerns, it should help you solve some problems, avoid others, and give you a head start on dealing with many more for a long time to come.

The book is divided into four parts. The first part (chapters 1–4) outlines general issues in parenting including how to think about your role as an adult and some very reliable principles of learning, behavior and motivation. I believe this section will help you to look at and think about the process of parenting in a different way. You can find instructions anywhere on how to do a Time-Out or Job Card Grounding, but understanding why these procedures work will get you a lot further than just following the blueprint. The second part of the book, chapter 5 builds on this foundation of knowledge, outlining six general steps for establishing greater structure, improved teaching methods, and better behavior within your family. The third part (chapters 6–8) is a sort of "tool box" in which you will find specific, often step-by-step methods for responding to your child's behavior. Finally, chapter 9 summarizes the previous sections and provides a ready resource for review and for reminding yourself of some of the key concepts and methods. I trust and hope that the ideas and methods will be as useful to you and your family as they have been to the families I have worked with over the years.

Walk Fast and Carry a Clipboard

J ust about all of my clients are children or adolescents, from the toddlers who have tantrums or refuse to sleep in their own beds to the teens who refuse to do homework or accidently forget to be home by curfew.

Most often, I expect to meet with them and their parents for only a handful of visits, generally for an hour or less each time. The rest of their time (the other one-hundred-sixty-seven hours in the week) is spent somewhere else, mostly at home or school, but certainly not at my office. What this means is that parents and teachers have a lot more time and many more opportunities to have an impact on these children than I ever could. For most children, it is parents and other adults who act as the "control system" in their lives—the organizing and supervising authority that supports them when they are doing well and gives them a little nudge when they get off track.

Parent and teacher influence continues long after I am just a distant memory. I am most helpful to the kids I work with when I act as a kind of coach or advisor to the adults with whom they spend the majority of their time for years on end. So, before we look more closely at how and why kids act the way they do, we probably should spend a little time talking about adult behavior— that is, how to act like a grown-up.

THE GROWN-UP JOB DESCRIPTION

Maybe the most important part of acting like a grown-up is to recognize that the ultimate goal is to put yourself out of a job, to get rid of your kids by helping them become successful adults. At a practical level, this means you help them learn and practice the basic life skills they will need no matter what walk of life they end up in, behaviors that will be useful to them now *and* later. Learning basic social skills such as introducing themselves or apologizing, for example, will help them get along better with family and friends now and with bosses and coworkers later on. Learning to handle frustration will help them tolerate annoying classmates today as well as rude drivers and inconsiderate colleagues later.

When you train them to work toward a long-term goal— such as toiling away at a big assignment for school—you prepare them to be persistent in working for college degrees, raises and promotions later on. Finally, when kids are taught to do what they *need* to do before doing what they *want* to do (such as finishing the dishes before turning on the television), they are more likely to be self-disciplined in their adult lives (paying off the credit cards before buying that new big screen television).

Acting like a grown-up also means you help your children develop a sense of confidence and competence by allowing them to confront some problems on their own, without interference from you. They should know you have enough faith in them to expect them to take responsibility for their own behavior. You demonstrate your confidence in them by allowing them to deal with some problems independently and not jumping in to manage everything for them.

> Maybe the most important part of acting like a grown-up is to recognize that the ultimate goal is to put yourself out of a job, to get rid of your kids by helping them become successful adults.

In fact, doing things for children that they are capable of doing for themselves is disrespectful to the children. When parents do this, the message these children get is that their parents do not trust them or believe they are capable of taking care of things on their own. Parents who do everything for their kids usually end up with kids who don't know how to do much for themselves.

If there is anything we know for sure about children, it is that they feel most safe and secure when the world around them is reliable and predictable. Of all the things that affect this sense of security for children, the behavior of their parents and other adults is the most important. When grown-ups act in consistent and predictable ways, kids are able to relax and just be kids. They don't have to spend a lot of time and energy trying to figure out how mom and dad might react to their behavior, because it's the same way their parents reacted the time before and the time before that.

Children really do want to believe grown-ups have a good idea about what's going on. Their lives are much easier if it seems to them that the adults around them know what should be done and can be counted on to do it. Do we always really know what's going on? I sure don't, but I don't think kids really need to know that. They have more than enough uncertainty and confusion to deal with without having our adult concerns piled on.

> You do not really have to know what you are doing all the time; just act like you do.

Children already get way too much information about all the wackiness in the world from the media and their friends. They do not need to hear about our financial worries and work hassles and their crazy Uncle Eddie's latest legal troubles. These are adult issues. Children do not need to be informed about them. They don't need to know that the world confuses and scares us sometimes too and that we would like to take a day or a month off from being a grown-up once in awhile.

What they need instead is to see parents who accept the authority and responsibility of adult life and who appear to have a plan for how to deal with things. You do not really have to know what you are doing all the time; just act like you do.

Back in my days as a professor of pediatrics, I used to advise my students on how to present themselves as they moved around the medical school campus. It can be summed up like this: "Walk fast and carry a clipboard." In other words, look like you know what you are doing. I found that if I had a clipboard with a few important looking papers on it and I was striding forward at a good pace, head up, eyes forward, I could go just about anywhere I wanted to on campus and no one would ask questions or challenge me. They assumed I had authority because I acted like I had authority. I think this is a good way to present yourself to your children. Look like you have a plan and a purpose, and your children will probably believe you do. Walk fast and carry a clipboard.

FRIENDLY SURE, BUT NOT A FRIEND

Most of us have heard many people say you should be your children's parent, not their friend. In fact, I might as well say it too. Here it is: *You should be your children's parent, not their friend.* But what exactly does this mean? Does it mean you should not be friendly with your children? Of course not. Does it mean you should not treat them with the same respect you would give one of your friends? Nope. Mostly it means that your children should be able to tell the difference between you and their friends, and not just because you are taller. They should be able to see that you behave, think, dress and talk differently. You act like a grown-up.

Treating your children with respect includes giving careful consideration to what they think and feel, but in the end, it should be clear to them that your opinion matters more. Here are some other ways you demonstrate you are a parent, not a friend. Your children should know that

- You will protect them, but not pamper them.

- You will be absolutely reliable in making sure they are safe and meeting their needs, but just as reliable in delivering discipline when they misbehave.

- You are willing to let them experience the discomfort and frustration of bad decisions, even when it is painful for you and you would really like to jump in and rescue them.

- You will work hard to make their lives fun and interesting and enjoyable, as long as they are doing what they are supposed to be doing.

- You trust them enough to let them explore and take risks, but you also care enough to stop them when they get dangerously close to the edge.

- You will try to do what is right for them, even when it is inconvenient or uncomfortable for them and you.

When children see that their parents are patient enough with them to allow them to try some things on their own and that parents value effort and persistence as much as the end result, they are likely to learn to take some pride in their work. If they can see their parents are not bothered or put off by failure, but look at it as only a temporary setback, they will learn to keep trying. If they know they will still be accepted and loved just as much even when they come up a little short, they will feel more confident about taking on the world and getting back up when they fall.

Not long ago, I was presenting a parenting workshop at an elementary school in my area. There were about a hundred or so parents in the audience. Sometime during the presentation, as

I usually do, I outlined some of the negative effects of allowing television in a child's room (inactivity, obesity, higher risk for smoking, sleep problems, weight problems, lower test scores) and suggested that parents go home that night and take the TV out of their kids' rooms.

A mother in the front row laughed and said something like, "Oh, sure that will happen." I asked her why she thought this would be so hard. "Because it's *his* TV," she said. It also turned out that, most nights, she was in the habit of lying down to watch television with him and sometimes fell asleep there herself. She probably should have made an appointment with my office the next day, because she is going to have some work to do.

This mother was so concerned about upsetting her child and so timid about asserting herself as a grown-up that it was unthinkable to her that she could make this simple change. She could not imagine doing something her child would dislike or depriving him of his favorite nighttime programs. Maybe she did not want to give up her own routine of watching television with him in his bedroom. Or maybe she was thinking about the tantrum he would throw when she unplugged the television. Whatever the reason, this was a clear case of too much friend, not enough parent.

Other parents react differently. In a recent movie about Ray Charles, the musician, there is a scene where he is still a boy and just coming to terms with his blindness. He trips and falls over a chair and lies on the floor, calling out for his mother to help him. His mother stands motionless on the other side of the room, trying to hold back her tears, but knowing that jumping in with too much help and too much sympathy would only make him weaker and more dependent, not stronger. This mother showed more understanding of her job as a parent than a roomful of so-called experts. She trusted him enough to allow him to rise up to meet his own challenges in his own way, with support, but not interference

IT'S A PROCESS, NOT AN EVENT

Kids should be expected to do what kids do. They are on their way to becoming adults, but not there yet. Adult knowledge and skills take a long time to learn, and the process does not always go along smoothly. It can be frustrating when children seem to be able or willing to do something one day and not the next. Just when we think some idea is finally soaking in, their brains seem to spring a leak.

What all of this adds up to is that acting like a grown-up means we understand parenting is a process, not an event. It takes time and consistency and persistence, and we don't even get to know for sure how they will turn out until years later when the kids grow up and move away. Some days are good, some days not so. Sometimes the progress and developing maturity are obvious and amazing. Some days we wonder if our kids will still be living in our basement decades from now.

> **Kids should be expected to do what kids do.**

Relax, it is normal for things to be different from one day to the next. The goal is to have them ready for adult life by the time they go off to college, not on the first day of kindergarten.

And while you're busy allowing your kids not to be perfect, you might want to give yourself a break too. You do not have to be the perfect parent. Just work on being a good enough parent and try to get better at it as you go. Show up and do the best you can with the circumstances of the day. Then go to bed, get up the next day and do it all over again.

WELCOME TO THE CLUB

Another part of acting like a grown-up has to do with our interactions with other grown-ups. Whether we want to or not, all of us belong to the same club, the adults club. What is important about this is that our kids already think of all adults as being members of the club. Their ideas about how to treat adults depend, in part, on how they see us treating and speaking about other adults. If they see us treating other adults with respect and courtesy (even when they do not seem to deserve it), children will believe this is the way things are supposed to be done.

On the other hand, if children hear us making negative comments about another adult or disrespecting appropriate adult authority, they will believe it is all right for them to treat adults that way too. That includes us. After all, if one member of the club is not worthy of respect, neither are the others.

Whenever a child hears us question the authority of any adult, we diminish our own authority with that child. If we are disrespectful to a teacher or a relative or an ex-husband, then all adults (including us) become a little smaller in that child's eyes. The child feels a little less secure, and our own job as a parent gets a little more difficult. As adults, we are bound to disagree with each other. But, like financial problems and Uncle Eddie's wayward behavior, our children do not need to know about this. Adult business is adult business and should be settled by adults out of earshot of the children.

In general, children should be encouraged to listen to their parents, their friends' parents, aunts and uncles, grandparents, teachers, principals, police officers, bus drivers and just about any adult in a position of legitimate authority. Obviously, we want to teach our kids there are some things they should not do just because an adult says so, but it is essential that they see us respecting appropriate authority and expecting them to do the same. If we want them to feel safe and secure, they need to believe that someone, somewhere knows what is going on and will tell them the right things to do.

If not trusted adults, then whom? If it looks like we cannot even agree about what is most important to them, how are children supposed to know whom to trust?

So, do we want to be friendly with our children? Of course. But if our children need us mainly to be their friends, they need to get out more. If we need them to be our friends, we need to get out more. Our job is to be parents. Protectors. Teachers. Cheerleaders. Coaches. Nurses. Chauffeurs. Teammates. It's a great job.

TWO

Four (or Maybe Five) Really Useful Principles of Behavior

A lot of parents tell me their children have a bad attitude. When I ask for some examples of bad attitude, they tell me about how their children do not do anything around the house, do not listen, have tantrums when told no and roll their eyes when parents are trying to explain something to them.

There probably really is a bad attitude in there somewhere, but what these parents are describing are behaviors—*actions* not attitudes. How would we know if the "bad attitude" improved? The children would help out around the house, would listen, would stay calm and would not roll their eyes. These are all changes in behavior.

I end up talking a lot about behavior in my office and when I do training or workshops. This does not mean ideas, attitudes and emotions are not important; of course they are. The thing is, we can't see thoughts or feelings. It is very difficult to explain them, teach them or even measure them in any accurate or reliable way. A lot of adults have a hard time understanding their own emotions very well. So how can we expect to be able to explain something to children (or have them explain it to us) when we don't really understand it ourselves? Is it really reasonable to tell children how they should feel about something or what their attitude should be? Can kids really just decide to change the way they feel anyway? You can see the problem.

It seems to me that what is most important is for our kids to *do* better. Thinking about spending more time practicing the saxophone will not make a child a better saxophone player, but practicing will. Feeling bad about coloring on the walls does not get the walls clean, scrubbing them does. Kids might tell us they know their math facts or spelling words, but we don't know for sure until we test them.

I have heard kids sincerely promise all kinds of things in my office, then go out and do something completely different. Sometimes, I tell the kids I work with that all their promises and good intentions *and* a dollar or two will buy them a can of soda. What I mean by this is that none of the words matter much until the behavior improves. Their future teachers and bosses will not give them a good grade or a raise based on good intentions; they will need to perform.

Ultimately, children's success depends a great deal on their behavior—what they are able to do and accomplish. More important, children who do better, feel better about themselves. Other people like being around them more. They develop a greater sense of confidence and competence and a more positive outlook because they are able to be more effective and people respond more positively to them. Improved behavior actually leads to more positive attitudes and emotions!

On the other hand, when children behave badly, life does not go well for them in a lot of ways. They develop fewer skills and do not accomplish as much. They have less to feel good about as a result. Other people do not want to be around them (at least not the kind of people you would want them to be around). Children who do not listen well at home tend not to get as much out of school because they are not used to being instructed or corrected by adults and do not accept this from their teachers (also members of the adults club) either. They lose confidence because their friends are making more progress than they are. They get pushed to the side socially. Behaving well is huge!

Being able to follow instructions from parents and teachers may be the most important foundational skill young children learn. Fortunately, we know some very useful rules for how behavior and learning work.

Imagine a group of kids playing basketball. Now pretend you know nothing about how basketball works (easy for me, since I really don't know that much about basketball). As you watch them play, you might think at first that it looks like a bunch of people just running back and forth in a kind of random way. But if you watch a while longer, you will start to figure the game out, even knowing little or nothing about it to start with.

> Improved behavior actually leads to more positive attitudes and emotions!

You will see that one group tries to get the ball in the hoop at one end, and the other group tries to stop them. You will see that you are supposed to bounce the ball when you walk or run with it. You will notice that people sweat a lot when they play this game, and so on. In other words, the patterns and rules will start to become clear. It won't seem quite as random.

Well, it turns out that the rules of behavior are not quite as simple, but they are very reliable. And the good news is that a whole lot of people who are a whole lot smarter than I am have spent a whole lot of time watching kids. As a result of all this time, attention and brainpower, we know some things about how kids learn and why they act the way they do.

REALLY USEFUL PRINCIPLE OF BEHAVIOR #1: MOST BEHAVIOR IS LEARNED BEHAVIOR

When babies come into the world, they do not do much. Eat. Sleep. Cry. Fill their diapers. That's about it. This means that everything else they do has to be learned. Everything. So all of the useful, helpful, productive behaviors such as walking, saying "please" and "thank you," doing homework, cleaning their rooms and paying their taxes are learned. No one is born knowing how to do any of these things.

Unfortunately, these are not the only behaviors kids learn along the way. A lot of other, not so attractive behaviors such as whining, hitting, pouting, messing up the toy room, and pretending to be sick to get out of going to school are also learned. What is important here is that all of these behaviors are learned in basically the same way. If we know something about how this happens (and we do), we can do a better job of teaching them what we want them to learn. We also can do a better job of *not* teaching them the things we would rather they not do. Sometimes, what we end up teaching is different from what we thought we were teaching.

Picture a young boy, maybe nine or ten years old. We will call him Joshua. He is watching television in the downstairs family room. His father comes to the top of the stairs and says, "Josh, time for bed. Turn off the TV, come upstairs, get ready and go to bed."

Josh says, "Okay, Dad."

What a great kid. But when Dad checks on him a few minutes later, Josh is still downstairs, still watching television. The volume of Dad's voice goes up a couple of notches. "Josh! I said it's time for bed. Turn off the TV, come upstairs and get to bed."

Again, Josh answers, "Okay, Dad."

Fabulous kid. But when Dad checks again a few minutes later, Josh has not budged. Still downstairs. Still watching television.

Now Dad yells at the top of his lungs, "Joshua! Turn off that TV, get in the bathroom, get ready and get to bed! Now!"

Josh turns off the television, comes upstairs, gets ready and goes to bed. I have told this story enough times to know that it will seem uncomfortably familiar to many of you.

What was learned here? What Dad learned is that Josh is a noncompliant child. Dad thinks he has to tell Josh three times before he will do anything. He has to yell or Josh will not listen. Dad thinks Josh has not learned much at all about how to follow directions. He probably will get more and more frustrated and yell louder and more often. As it turns out, Josh really has learned quite a bit from his father, just not what his father thought he was teaching. What Josh has learned is this:

- Dad is not serious until he starts to yell.

- When Dad starts to yell (here is the important part), he is ready to *do something* to me if I do not listen.

It was the fact that Dad was finally ready to do something that got Josh up the stairs and into bed. The yelling was only a signal to Josh that something bad was about to happen to him if he did not listen. His father had trained Josh to wait until he is yelling before listening to him! It was really the "bad thing about to happen" that caused Josh to get moving, not the yelling.

Other kids learn different signals that their parents are about to do something if they don't listen. Some know it is time to listen when their parents call them by their middle name or when they raise an eyebrow or when the parent gets up off the couch and starts coming toward them.

I would tell Josh's dad that it is important for him to be ready to do something (give a consequence) the first time if Josh does not listen. If he does, I would just about guarantee that Josh's hearing would improve and that they would get along better.

Just about every child learns some annoying behavior at some point. Even so-called normal children are difficult at times. So having a child with some problem behavior does not necessarily mean you have done something wrong, though often the behaviors that annoy us most (like not coming when called to come to bed) are the behaviors we have taught

> If children already knew how to do everything on their own or correct their own problem behavior, they would not need parents.

them. But just because annoying behavior is normal doesn't mean it should not be corrected.

If children already knew how to do everything on their own or correct their own problem behavior, they would not need parents. When problem behaviors come up, think of these times as teaching opportunities—your chance to show your kids what kinds of behaviors will not work for them and to teach them a better way to get what they want. Which leads us to the next rule of behavior.

REALLY USEFUL PRINCIPLE OF BEHAVIOR #2: BEHAVIOR IS MOTIVATED (IT SERVES A PURPOSE)

People do things for a reason, for two main reasons, actually. You probably are reading this book because you hope I have at least some idea of what I am talking about and you will gain one or two useful insights about kids. This is the first kind of motivator: Getting something you want. You hope to get some new parenting skills or a different way to look at your child's behavior by reading this book.

People go to work because they get paid. They go into the kitchen because they can get tasty snacks there. They have tantrums because it gets people to pay attention to them or to let them have their own way. All of these are behaviors that result in some kind of reward or payoff. All of them get the person something they want.

The other main reason for people to do things is this: getting out of something you do not want. Suppose you are driving just a little over the speed limit (not that you would ever actually do this, of course). You see a police car. You probably will do "stepping on the brake" behavior. Why? To keep something bad from happening. You slow down to keep from getting a ticket. Pretending to be sick to get out of going to school, whining or complaining to get out of doing chores and walking on the other side of the street to avoid a bully are other examples. In the bedtime example, Josh got up, got ready and went to bed because he wanted to avoid whatever bad thing his father was about to do if he did not.

Children can be counted on to try out all kinds of different behaviors. It's their job, really. The behaviors they keep doing or do more of are the ones that either get them something they want or get them out of something they do not want. In psychology, we call this being reinforced. If your child continues to do some behavior, good or bad, you can be sure it is being reinforced somehow. If it keeps being reinforced, it will keep happening.

Pay Attention to What You Pay Attention To

For most younger children, one item stands out above everything else on the list of reinforcers, or things they want. It's better than chocolate, better than the latest toy, television program or electronic gadget. It's even better than sugar or money. It's you. From the very beginning, children work hard to get attention from their parents. At first, they just cry and carry on until someone responds to them.

But as soon as they can focus their eyes, they learn to make eye contact. They learn to smile and coo and flirt with us. This happens in part because we are social creatures and we need to connect with each other. It also happens because humans develop very slowly. Babies and young children cannot get along on their own. They need adults to protect them and feed them and change their diapers. If they are not successful at getting the attention of caregivers, they cannot survive. Getting adults to pay attention to them is serious business to young children.

What this means is that, for just about all young kids, attention is a big reinforcer—maybe the biggest of all. It's something they are willing to work for. Think about all the times have you seen a child at the beach or a playground waving their hands and saying, "Look at me" or something similar. How many times has your own child brought you some picture or project they have been working on and tapped on your arm until you looked at it? Attention matters. Whatever you pay attention to is what you will get more of.

> Whatever you pay attention to is what you will get more of.

- If sticking out their tongue gets a big reaction from you, they will stick out their tongue more.

- If hitting themselves or having a tantrum gets your attention (even if it is just to try to stop them from doing it), they will probably do these behaviors more.

- If whimpering and whining at bedtime gets you to lie down with them, count on more whimpering and whining.

- If following directions, picking up toys or putting dirty dishes in the sink gets a big reaction, they will do these behaviors more.

- On the other hand, if doing any of these things results in your either ignoring or punishing the child in some way, they will do them less.

Here are the general rules about attention, especially for younger children:

- Attention is good.

- Positive attention is better than negative attention.

- Negative attention is better than no attention at all.

Several years ago, I attended a party at a relative's home. There were a lot of adults and kids there, with most of the adults seated in the living room. At one point, a young man, maybe five or six years old, started to make his way around the room, stopping in front of each adult. Sometimes he stuck out his tongue or made a grotesque face. Sometimes he made a rude noise. Each time he did this, the adult laughed or made some comment about how funny the child was, and he moved on to the next person.

Eventually, he got to me. He stretched his mouth out with his fingers and rolled his eyes up. I turned away. He walked around me until he was in front of me again, then made a series of obnoxious sounds. I turned away again.

From across the room, I heard his mother say, "Leave him alone, Alex. I don't think he likes kids." Now, I would be surprised if there was anyone in the room that day who likes kids more than I do. But I was not about to contribute to Alex's idea that these behaviors were "cute" by paying attention to them. I did not want to reinforce his inappropriate behavior. It was not my place to punish him, so I did the next best thing. I ignored him.

Every other adult in the room had encouraged him to be more obnoxious by how they responded to him. Because I really do like kids, even obnoxious ones, I refused to play.

Some children actually choose to do behaviors that get their parents to scold them or yell at them. If they find this is the most consistent way or the only way for them to get attention, they will do it. After all, negative attention is better than no attention at all. Anyone who works with children has seen examples of kids doing really extreme things just to get some kind of reaction out of a parent or other adult.

The take-home point here is that we want to try hard to notice good behavior when it happens and let them know we appreciate it. We want our kids to know that the best way to get our attention is by doing what they are supposed to do. Do not miss a chance to tell your children, young or old, what they are doing right.

REALLY USEFUL PRINCIPLE OF BEHAVIOR #3: CHILDREN LEARN BEST FROM WHAT HAPPENS TO THEM

It still amazes me every time I see an adult talking to a three-year-old child as if the child could understand adult concepts. Trying to explain complicated ideas about behavior or social rules to a young child is like trying to explain algebra, Russian literature or organic chemistry to them. They are not going to get it. They just are not ready yet. We are not surprised or upset when a three-year-old cannot seem to grasp algebra, but somehow we expect them to know why they behave the way they do, even if none of the adults around them can figure it out. Children, especially young children, learn best from what happens to them, not what we tell them.

"Now, Megan," Mom says to her four-year-old daughter, "do you understand why you can't act like that on the playground? What were you thinking? No one will ever want to play with you. They won't want to come over to your house. They won't want to be your friends. You will never get into a good college." (Okay, the last one is a bit of an exaggeration, but not much.)

Then Mom says something like, "Do you understand what I am telling you?"

Megan nods her head solemnly and seems to agree with what Mom says, but only because she has learned that nodding her head solemnly will get Mom to stop lecturing her, not because she really understands or really agrees with what Mom is talking about. Nodding her head allows her to escape from an unpleasant lecture (Really Useful Principle of Behavior #2). Mom believes that Megan has really learned something this time and lets her off the hook, increasing the chances for more head nodding behavior later on.

> Children, especially young children, learn best from what happens to them, not what we tell them.

The same kind of thing happens when parents demand that their kids tell them why they did something. Most often, the kid has no more idea than the parent does and probably less. Often, the real answer is, "Because I wanted to," but that usually does not go over too well with parents. When the child says, "Because I wanted to," the parent probably will get upset and insist that the child come up with some more profound explanation. Eventually, the child will figure out how to answer in the way the parent wants to hear. Mostly, what this child has learned is that it may be best not to answer truthfully if you want to stay out of trouble.

The main tool kids have for figuring out the world is their behavior. They try behaviors out and see what happens. Watch a toddler in a new place. Do they sit down, fold their hands and wait for someone to explain things to them? No. They move around and explore. They crawl under, over and around furniture and people. They look at objects, pick them up, turn them upside down, shake them, smell them, flip them over, throw them.

They are made to learn from their experiences, and they can't learn much if there is nothing going on. So, one other important rule that guides child behavior is this: If a situation is boring, find a way to make it interesting. Stir things up. Make something happen. It's their job. They are good at it. Our job is to try to make life more interesting for them when they are behaving well and more dull, boring, and uninteresting when they are behaving badly.

Sometimes, adults are tempted to think this rule no longer applies just because their children have gotten older and smarter and can discuss things more intelligently. By the time they get to middle school, most kids can reason about as well as their parents. But even though they have new ways to learn and understand doesn't mean the old ways stop working.

Did you stop enjoying positive experiences or dreading painful ones just because you became a grown-up? Talking about a boat ride may be enjoyable, but is nowhere near as good as getting out on the lake and feeling the spray on your face. Being scolded by your boss may make an impression on you, but the threat of being fired brings it home. In the same way, talking to your child about your concerns for their behavior is nowhere near as good as demonstrating your concern by making something happen. Of course you should take advantage of your child's developing cognitive and verbal skills, but not at the expense of meaningful action.

Be Like Gravity

Maybe the best illustration of how kids learn from experience is gravity. I could take just about any three- or four-month-old child up to the edge of the tallest building in town, and the child would roll off the edge without giving it a second thought. Yet just a few months later, the same child would back away from the edge.

How do they learn this? Do their parents sit them down and explain why it is a bad idea to jump off buildings? How many toddlers have had a class in physics? Yet every normally developing child learns not to jump off really tall objects. How? They learn from what happens to them. Because from the first time they can lift their wobbly little heads, they feel the effects of gravity, and gravity is a wonderful teacher.

What makes gravity such a good teacher? First, it is absolutely reliable. If you jump off a building ten times, you will fall down ten times. Never up. Never sideways. You will always accelerate at the same rate as you fall. Gravity does not give warnings or explanations. It does not give second chances. It does not yell or get angry, it just happens. As a result of this, kids accept it and change their behavior accordingly. They do not get mad at gravity or argue with it, they just take it as a fact of life. This is how we want to be when we deliver negative consequences to kids. Like gravity. A force of nature.

REALLY USEFUL PRINCIPLE OF BEHAVIOR #4: THE LEARNING PROCESS

We know now that most behavior is learned. We know that behavior is motivated. We know that children learn best from what happens to them, not what we tell them. So how do we take advantage of these rules of behavior to teach children more effectively?

It seems to me that the best thing we can do for our kids to help them learn to make good choices. We want them to choose to behave in ways that are appropriate and productive. We want our children to develop skills and habits that will help them succeed later in life. When they are small, we make most of the choices for our children. If we need to, we can make them do what we want (though I have seen two-year-olds whose parents didn't seem to be able to make them do much of anything). We can take their little hands in ours and make them scrub the crayon marks off the wall. The problem is that they get bigger and stronger and faster, and we don't.

As they grow and develop, children spend more and more time away from us at school and in outside activities. It gets harder just to keep up with them and harder still to make them do things they may not want to do. But this does not mean we can't continue to teach and encourage our kids to make good choices. We do this by first demonstrating as clearly as we can what choices will work best for them, then repeating the lesson over and over until it sinks in. These two ideas, contrast and repetition, are the main tools we use to guide our children toward good decisions and good behavior. Both are required to create successful learning situations. Both are necessary, but neither is enough by itself.

Contrast

We encourage good choices by what we make happen in our kids' world depending on their behavior. If they make good choices (behaviors we like), we want to try to find ways to make their lives as fun, interesting and enjoyable as we are able. When they make bad choices (behaviors we do not like), we want to make their lives change in a noticeable and unpleasant way, to make their lives as dull, boring and uncomfortable as possible.

The bigger the difference between these outcomes, the easier their choice is. This is the idea of contrast. If there is no difference in what happens to them regardless of the choices they make, there is no contrast. In other words, if you don't act different, they won't act different. But if there is a noticeable difference in what happens when they choose one kind of behavior over another, there is contrast, and they are more likely to learn what we want. In general, the greater the contrast, the quicker the learning.

Picture two preschool-age children playing together, having a good time with building blocks (you know, the little kind you are always stepping on or sucking up into the vacuum). An argument develops. Mother overhears the argument from the next room. She walks in and says, "What's going on in here?"

The two children come up with two different explanations of what happened, competing with each other and shouting to get their points across. Since mother is not clear about what is going on or who might be at fault, she just tells them they need to play nicely and leaves the room. What changed for them? Not much. Mother interrupted their argument briefly, then they went right back to playing, right back to their fun, interesting and enjoyable activity. Mother's response to their inappropriate behavior produced little or no meaningful contrast. My guess is it won't be long before another fight erupts. No contrast, no learning.

Now picture the same two children in the same situation. Same argument. Same mother walks into the same room and says, "We are not going to argue about blocks." She tells the children to put the blocks back into a plastic storage bin and supervises while this happens. Then, she does not allow the blocks to come out again for the rest of the day. In this case, the children went immediately from an enjoyable activity (playing with blocks) to a not-so-enjoyable activity (picking up blocks) when they argued. A very noticeable difference. Lots of contrast and a positive learning experience.

In the first example, mother actually encouraged more arguing by asking what was going on. She put herself in the middle of the disagreement. She set herself up as the person to come to resolve every conflict. Chances are she will hear more complaining, whining and tattling.

In the second example, she taught another kind of lesson in a much more effective way. She made something happen.

She created a different outcome, a prompt and meaningful consequence. Like gravity. She delivered the message that her children should work on solving their own disagreements because it will be painful for both of them when they do not. Chances are they will begin to learn to settle some of their own arguments, and they should be trusted to do this.

Lack of contrast shows up in a few other ways. Some parents are distracted or even disinterested, and their involvement in child or family activities is minimal. These parents tend to be very tolerant of their children's behavior because they do not want to be bothered. Problem behaviors are seen mainly as "inconvenient," and the parents actively avoid dealing with them. In fact, much of the time, there is little reaction of any kind toward the children, regardless of whether they are behaving well or badly. Discipline and teaching are infrequent and inconsistent.

On the rare occasion when the kids in these families get into trouble, they might be put in Time-Out or sent to their rooms where they are, you guessed it, ignored. What really changes when this happens? Location, but not much else. They were being ignored outside their rooms and continued to be ignored in their rooms. Not much contrast and very little productive learning.

At the other extreme are parents who are over involved in their children's lives. The needs and desires of the children come first in these families. The parents are attentive to every detail of their children's lives, but have few rules or expectations for them. Instead, they rely on reasoning and consultation with the children.

Kids in these families get lots of praise and privileges, no matter what their behavior has been like. Punishment is rare and children are allowed to manage their own activities for the most part. Discipline usually involves being "talked to" or even "yelled at," but not much really changes for them when they misbehave. There is no more contrast here than in the previous example.

We would expect children in this situation to develop a sense of entitlement. They get used to having what they want when they want it, even when they misbehave. These children tend to become very upset when their needs are not met. They have a difficult time handling frustration because they get so little practice at it.

Finally, some parents are more rigid in their interactions with children. They emphasize obedience without question in every circumstance. There is little consideration given to the nature and needs of the children when making decisions. Parental rules are excessive or unreasonable, and punishment is frequent, harsh or unpredictable. These parents tend to focus mostly on what the child does wrong. Criticism and statements of dissatisfaction with the children are common, regardless of how they have behaved. There is little contrast and what contrast there is happens inconsistently (no repetition).

Children in this situation may focus mostly on finding ways to avoid the parent. Later on, when the child feels more able to challenge the parent directly, rebellion is a common response.

Repetition

Several years ago I saw Anthony in my office. He was maybe six or seven years old at the time. After talking to him for a few minutes, I asked him to play with toys in another part of the room while I spoke with his mother.

After a few minutes, he walked over to us and showed his mother a toy train he had been playing with. She said something like, "Oh, isn't that cute! It has stickers on the side and the engineer's head moves when the wheels go around." Then she sent him back to play again.

A few minutes later, the boy approached his mother again with another toy. This time, she responded angrily, "Would you get away from me, I'm talking to the doctor!"

There was plenty of contrast (though not in the way we would want). What was missing was the second important part of effective teaching, repetition. Repetition means responding to similar behaviors in a similar way. In this example, the same behavior, approaching mom with a toy, produced two much different responses, the opposite of repetition.

Suppose you wanted to teach your daughter some geography facts. The first time, you tell her the capital of Texas is Dallas. The next time, you tell her the capital is Austin. Then Houston. Then Abilene. San Antonio. Omaha. Kalamazoo. It would take a long time for your daughter to learn the real capital if she gets different and conflicting information each time. There is no repetition.

Imagine how frustrating this would be. What if someone gave you a different set of directions to the same place each time you asked? Different rules each time you played the same game? That is really what was happening to the young man with the toy train. Mother had two wildly different reactions to the same behavior by the child. No repetition. No learning. One mixed up little boy.

Inconsistency is not always so obvious. Picture a mom who is on the telephone when her daughter asks her a question. One time, she answers the child right away. The next time, in the same situation, she says something like, "You will have to wait a minute, honey, I'm on the phone."

Same situation, two different reactions, though not as extreme as the previous example. I have seen this in a number of classrooms as well. A child might get the teacher's attention by raising a hand, standing by the teacher's desk, saying the teacher's name out loud, or tapping her on the shoulder. At other times, the child gets corrected or disciplined for some of the very same behaviors.

Students in these classes tend to be unruly and noisy. When there are no routines in a household or classroom; when rules are enforced sometimes, but not others; when parents or teachers react differently in the same situation from one day to the next, children struggle to figure out what they are supposed to do. They are not getting the kind of consistent feedback they need to help them judge which behaviors are acceptable. Worse, when adults get angry and upset with the child for doing something that was okay the day before, the child can be thrown off balance emotionally as well as behaviorally.

Children show us how important repetition is to them in a number of ways. For example, how many times have you wanted to pull your hair out because your daughter or son wanted to watch the same video or TV show over and over again or play the same board game time after time? In fact, some children's shows now repeat the exact same program every day for a solid week for this reason. They recognize the importance of repletion to learning. They know their viewers learn a little more and feel a little more competent with each showing.

Repetition matters. It is the most powerful variable in learning and essential to effective discipline and motivation. Chances are that if you do not have some kind of a plan for dealing with child behavior, you will not be consistent, and repetition and learning will suffer.

THE MOST IMPORTANT PRINCIPLE OF BEHAVIOR AND LEARNING

Repetition and consistency are the basis for successful behavioral training, but they are even more important for another reason. Reliable and predictable behavior by parents provides the foundation for emotional stability in their children. Children feel more secure when they know what to expect. In fact, if you were looking for a way to make most kids (and most adults, for that matter) uncomfortable or anxious, it would be to make things as unpredictable and inconsistent as possible.

Think about how you feel when something unpredictable happens to you. Your car won't start. Someone does not show up to meet you when they are supposed to. You get an unexpectedly bad grade or get laid off from a job. It is upsetting, isn't it? It's the same for kids. Children count on adults to help them figure out the important things about life, and they learn this mostly from what happens to them and around them (Really Useful Principle of Behavior #3). When parents act in inconsistent and unpredictable ways, it is confusing and upsetting to their children.

One big difference between adults and children is that we adults have adult skills to help us get back in control when unexpected events happen. If my car won't start, I have a cell phone and a credit card. I can call someone and get help. I can try out my limited mechanical skills to get it going again.

Children do not have adult skills or resources. What they have is their behavior. They try out some behavior or another and see what happens. If it seems to them that something good happens as a result, they will be more likely to do that behavior again in the future (Really Useful Principle of Behavior #2). If something bad happens, they will do that behavior less. If adults don't respond to their behavior in the same way from one time to the next, they will be

> Reliable and predictable behavior by parents provides the foundation for emotional stability in their children.

confused and often will escalate their behaviors to try to get the grown-ups to react in some predictable way. Sometimes, getting a *consistent* response from a parent is even more important to kids than getting a *positive* response. It is hard to figure out where you are going in the world when the person you rely on most gives you different directions each time you ask.

Everyone has heard that you should be consistent with your children. Now you know why. This means that one of our primary guiding principles for parents is to respond to children in a consistent way. If you have not spent time thinking about how you will deal with your child's behavior, if you do not have a plan, you probably won't be consistent. Your child should have a pretty good idea about how you will react to a situation before it happens because you have a pretty good idea first.

THREE

Four (Really, Only Four) Important Distinctions

IMPORTANT DISTINCTION #1:
EDUCATION VS. TRAINING

Suppose you wanted to teach me to play the piano. You might talk to me about how to play the piano, showing me diagrams and explaining everything carefully from beginning to end. I would eventually learn to label all the keys with the right notes and be able to tell you what each of the pedals does, but this doesn't mean I could play the piano. I would be educated, but not trained.

Anyone who works with children knows for sure that education is important. In fact, educating children and parents is a big part of my job. But education has its limits. Behavioral skills must be trained, not just explained.

The best way to train behavior is through what we do. Talking too much during disciplinary interactions is a trap many parents fall into. Often, the kids know exactly what they are supposed to do; they just don't do it. Explaining it to them for the five-hundred-first time does not make them any more likely to do it than they were after the first five hundred times you explained it. When it comes to teaching through discipline, it is best to stay focused on action. Talk less, act more. You might say the best way to help your kids see the light is to let them feel the heat. Save the discussions for later.

All too often, adults make the mistake of thinking that, if they just explain what should be done, the child will do it. Some schools have whole "discipline" systems built around having children fill out forms describing what they did wrong and outlining what they should do differently the next time. A lot of kids I know can fill out these forms perfectly for the same offense time after time after time. But then they keep making the same mistake. They are educated, but not trained. They know what to do, but they don't do it. This really isn't discipline at all; it's continuing education. The students have graduate-level skills in filling out forms, but the problem behavior does not change. The situation is not likely to improve much until there is more emphasis on training.

Training involves doing and experiencing, not being lectured, nagged or having a discussion. If I want to learn how to play the piano, I need to play the piano. I need to hear the unpleasant sounds when I play the wrong notes and the sweet tones when I play the right ones. I need to experience the consequences of my behavior and to see what happens as I change what I do. More information does not help much, but more practice does.

At times, parents have to do things for (or to) their children that cannot be explained to them at all. You can't explain to an infant why you allow their pediatrician to give them painful shots. There is no way to make a toddler truly understand why it is dangerous to run into the street or stick a fork in the electrical outlet. We might use the word *dangerous* to describe these behaviors, but a toddler really does not understand

> When it comes to teaching through discipline, it is best to stay focused on action. Talk less, act more.

what this means. Still, their lack of understanding does not keep us from doing what we need to do to protect their safety.

Even though children do gain more knowledge and understanding as they mature, there are still a huge number of things they just will not understand until they become adults. Trying to explain the adult world to a child is like trying to explain snow to someone who has lived his or her entire life in the tropics. They can get the general idea, but the reality is much more complicated.

By definition, children have not lived in the adult world yet. Their understanding is limited by their experience and point of view, and no amount of talk will bridge the gap. The fact that they don't understand why we adults do some of the things we do should not keep us from doing the right thing. Some things (such as picking up your room or paying your taxes) have to be done just because they have to be done, just because you said so.

IMPORTANT DISTINCTION #2:
JUMPING IN VS. JUMPING AHEAD

Parents have lots of responsibilities, none of them more important than keeping their children safe. When kids are tiny and helpless, we have to protect them from everything, because they cannot protect themselves from anything. We arrange our homes and activities to make sure our children are not exposed to potentially harmful objects or events. We put up gates, lock doors, and strap them into car safety seats. We give them vitamins and dress them warmly when it is cold outside. We keep medicines and chemicals out of reach. This is "jumping in."

> When kids are tiny and helpless, we have to protect them from everything, because they cannot protect themselves from anything.

Jumping in happens when we put ourselves between our kids and experiences that might injure them or be too upsetting or difficult for them. This is absolutely appropriate when children are little and unable to protect themselves, but as they grow and mature, this should start to change.

Obviously, we always try to protect children from situations that might truly harm them. Even so, over time we gradually allow them to have experiences that might be a little painful or uncomfortable, but may teach them something important. Often, we can see these things coming, and the temptation is to jump in and save them.

The problem with jumping in too much is that children who rarely experience the discomfort or pain of their own bad choices tend to become more and more reckless in their behavior. They think nothing bad will ever happen to them no matter how they behave. They also tend to have very little ability to tolerate frustration or work through a difficult situation because they are used to having problems solved quickly for them.

There is a great deal of learning in making the wrong choice and experiencing the negative consequences of that choice. When parents jump in and protect their children from every inconvenience or discomfort, they are depriving the child of that learning. A skinned knee or two does a better job of convincing a child to be careful on his or her bike than a lecture on bike safety ever could.

> Sometimes, the best thing to do for your child is nothing.

Sometimes, children come to resent the parent who jumps into every situation. They see the parent as intrusive and controlling, or embarrassing them in front of friends. Other kids in this situation decide there is no need for self control because the parent will clean up whatever messes they make in their lives. I see this happen with toddlers who never have to pick up after themselves all the way up to adolescents whose parents continue to battle with the school or the legal system to help their kid avoid richly deserved consequences.

Sometimes, the best thing to do for your child is nothing. The parent who recognizes that a child is about to make a mistake, realizes that the consequence will be painful (but not harmful) and allows the child to go ahead, is practicing "jumping ahead."

Instead of reacting in the moment, the parent looks forward and understands the value of the learning experience for the child. This parent sees that a little bit of pain now will save the child from much more pain later (just like getting shots from the doctor).

This can be hard for some parents, but when we jump into situations just because we do not want to see our kids get hurt (but not injured), we are acting mostly to protect our own feelings. Sometimes, parents themselves have to deliver the painful consequences that make it clear to the child that a bad choice has been made. Sometimes we just have to let nature take its course. Remember: the idea is to *protect,* but not *pamper.*

IMPORTANT DISTINCTION #3: ACTIVE NONCOMPLIANCE VS. PASSIVE NONCOMPLIANCE

At times, kids are very open about the fact that they do not plan to listen to their parents. When asked to do something, they say, "No." This kind of openly defiant behavior is what we would call *active noncompliance.* A lot of kids do this at some point. Toddlers and preschoolers seem to be particularly fond of this approach.

One of my all-time favorite patients was Isaiah, a second grader who visited with me at a teaching clinic. Several of my graduate students were observing me working with the family from the other side of a two-way mirror.

I told the Isaiah to pick up some blocks he had gotten out. He refused. I put him in Time-Out, released him after a couple of minutes, then told him again to pick up the blocks. He refused again and went back to Time-Out. When I got him out this time, he stood up straight, threw his shoulders back, crossed his arms and said, "Face it, I'm not picking them up." What a great kid!

I could hear shouts of laughter from the students on the other side of the observation window. There was no doubt about what needed to happen with this little guy. It took a couple more trips to the Time-Out chair, but I made sure he picked up the blocks. Then, just to reinforce the point, I dumped the blocks out and had him pick them up again. This time, he picked them up without any argument or complaint, and I was sure we understood each other. We got along well from that time on.

In some ways, this kind of active noncompliance is easier to deal with because you know what you are up against. There was nothing sneaky or underhanded about Isaiah. He was clear about his intentions. Most parents will not tolerate this kind of overt defiance and will usually take prompt and forceful action to deal with it. If they don't, the child will learn to simply refuse any time he or she does not feel like doing something. It happens.

Most kids, though, learn quickly that active noncompliance— or just plain refusing to do what their parents tell them—is not such a good idea because most parents do not like this and will react quickly, usually in an unpleasant way. So they try a different approach. Instead of refusing to do what they are told, they agree to do it, just not right away.

Remember Josh, the boy who did not want to come upstairs to get ready for bed? He was good at this. Like a lot of kids, he understood that his parents were much less likely to make him listen if he seemed to be going along. Father said, "Come up to bed now," and Josh said, "Okay." He just didn't do it. The words were right, but the behavior was wrong. This is *passive noncompliance.* This happens often.

A lot of kids learn that if they seem agreeable, but then drag their feet for a while, they get out of having to do things at least some of the time. Maybe they say they will get to it right after supper or as soon as they get to the next level on their video game or tomorrow. They know that at least sometimes their parents get distracted and forget they asked them to do something. At the very least, there is a good chance they will get to do what they want for a little while longer before they have to listen. And, even if the parent eventually reminds them, they can just say they forgot and probably not get into trouble. Not a bad strategy, really.

This is one of those times where being casual about parenting can lead to bigger problems. The main thing children learn from this situation is to put off doing whatever needs to be done. They learn to be sneakier. This is probably not exactly what the parent had in mind.

Sometimes passive noncompliance looks a little different. Just about every parent has heard their child claim they can't do something when the parent knows perfectly well they can. Often, children learn there is some benefit to having a parent think they can't do something. Sometimes children learn that saying they can't do something means they will not have to. Sometimes they learn that saying "I can't" or "I need you to help me" will get a parent to do it for them or spend a lot of one-on-one time with them trying to help them.

Madison and her family came into one of my teaching clinics in a pediatrician's office. She was in second or third grade at the time. Unfortunately, this young girl had some developmental delays and could not talk. Madison had no spoken language at all. Her parents told me she could not follow directions because of her lack of speech. I suggested that maybe we should test this idea out. I asked Madison to hand a wooden puzzle piece to her father. She gave me a blank stare and did nothing. So I put her in Time-Out. When I let her out and told her again to hand the puzzle piece to her father, she did it right away.

Madison had not been following instructions because no one was insisting she follow instructions. She had learned that if she just gave a blank look and stalled for a while, she would not have to do anything. This youngster had missed out on a lot of learning opportunities because everyone assumed she could not do what was asked of her, so they just stopped asking. When she did follow my instruction, her parents were amazed, and I looked a lot smarter than I actually am.

It is easy to forget that our children are growing, developing and learning every day. We are around them all the time, and sometimes their new abilities sneak up on us. They are always acquiring new skills, learning to do things they really could not do just a few months or days or even a few hours before. We always want to keep challenging them, to keep asking them to do a little more than they, or even we, might think they are capable of. We want to give them reasons to keep trying to do more.

Here is the take-home point. Active noncompliance and passive noncompliance may look different, but they produce exactly the same result. The child does not do what the parent said. Any time this happens, the child is getting practice with not listening. The seeds of a habit of a noncompliance are being planted and cultivated. Whether active or passive, *all noncompliance* should result in an assertive and immediate response from parents. In the chapters that follow, we will look at several specific ways to respond to this kind of situation.

IMPORTANT DISTINCTION #4: CAN'T DO VS. WON'T DO

Kids do not always accomplish everything we want them to. Obviously. There are two main reasons for this. The first is what we might call the "can't do" issue. Sometimes, people truly are not able to do what is asked of them. Something about their makeup or circumstances keep them from being able to do it. For example, there is no chance I ever will be a major league baseball player. Never mind the fact that I am now too (ahem) mature. I have never had the physical ability to play ball at that level and never will. No amount of training or practice, no promised reward will get me to do it. I can't. I also will not be spending six months next year on a luxury cruise in the Caribbean (unless I get hired on as a cabin boy). My situation does not allow me to do this. I can't afford it. I might really like to do it, but I can't. No amount of encouragement will change this. No threatened or actual punishment will get me there.

Can't Do Problems

We all know there are some things kids can't do. They can't perform open heart surgery. They can't run a mile in less than four minutes or complete firefighter training. They can't grow beards. Since no one really expects children to do surgery, put out fires, or grow beards, it is not much of a problem when they can't. But, for some kids, the can't do items are more basic and more serious. They can't learn to read. They can't stay focused. They can't moderate their emotions. No matter how hard we try to motivate them, they can't. I know a lot of children who have some kind of "can't do" problem. For these children, we may have to adjust our expectations or help them find other ways to reach their goals. Just encouraging them to try harder or punishing them for not performing will not work.

As we think about what we should expect from our children, it is important that we have a good idea what they are actually capable of. If we continue to insist our children do things they truly can't do, conflict and damaged relationships are sure to follow.

Imagine if, day after day, your boss demanded that you do a job you had never been trained for and did not understand. What if you were threatened with being fired every day for not doing the job, but there was never any effort to teach you the skills needed to do it? How much would you look forward to going to work? What would you think about your boss?

Sometimes, "can't do" problems happen when the child does have the aptitude or capacity to do what is asked but simply has not learned how yet. Suppose I ask a bright twelve-year-old boy to keep official score at a baseball game, but he has never seen a score book before. He is capable, but can't do what is asked because he does not know how. This kind of "can't do" problem is referred to as a skill deficit. In this case, we try to figure out what skill is missing and the best way to teach it. I would not punish the young man for not keeping the baseball score correctly. I would teach him how to do it.

Sometimes we only need to teach some specific skill such as how to operate the washing machine, how to add single-digit numbers or how to sweep a floor. Some children are missing more general and more serious items like social skills, organizational skills, frustration tolerance or self calming skills. These things are much more complicated and harder to teach, but the main issue is the same: missing but trainable skills.

A second kind of "can't do" problem happens because the child is not old enough or mature enough to do what is asked. They just have not grown into the job yet. For example, it would not be reasonable to expect three year olds to make all their own meals without help or five year olds to do the dishes by themselves. A nine-year-old child, even one with good math skills, should not be expected to balance the family checkbook and even a talented thirteen-year-old probably should not be trusted to fill out our income tax forms.

We want to make sure the tasks we assign are appropriate to the child's age or stage of development. If not, we either have to change our expectations to fit their developmental level or allow time for the child to grow and mature.

Finally, some children have disabilities or disorders that make it difficult or impossible to do tasks most other children their age can do. They appear to be making an effort, but just can't seem to do what is asked of them. For them, we first want to consider the nature of the disability or disorder and whether it can be treated directly. We may have to adjust our expectations to fit their capabilities or find other ways to accommodate their condition. This is a situation where you probably want to have some help from a professional. The point is that we have to know enough about what typical development looks like and about our own kids to be confident they are up to the tasks we ask them to perform.

Won't Do Problems

At the same time, it is important that we not be too quick to decide a child can't do something. I have had any number of parents who told me their children could not sit still, could not follow directions, could not sleep in their own bed, could not eat vegetables, or could not stay dry all night. All of these are problems that can be fixed relatively easily much of the time.

Sometimes parents decide a child can't do something and just stop asking. This often happens when children have had some kind of medical or developmental problem. Parents get used to not making demands on the child, and the child gets used to letting someone else do all the work. Often, children in this situation learn to put more effort into getting other people to do things for them than into trying to do things for themselves. They have been trained to be helpless, or at least to act helpless.

"Can't do" problems happen. But the other and much more common reason kids do not do what we want them to is this: They don't feel like it. For whatever reason, kids sometimes decide it is not worth it to them to make the effort to do what they are told. We might call this the "won't do" problem. Children might have all the knowledge, skill and resources they need to do the task, but since they do not want to do it, they don't. I have yet to meet a kid who did not have at least some "won't do" in them.

Here's the thing. It is not possible to deal with the "can't do" problems until we deal with the "won't do" problems. In fact, we have no way of knowing what someone is capable of doing if they do not really try. How can we measure what does not happen? We cannot tell how many math problems someone can do if they won't pick up a pencil. We cannot be sure how many jumping jacks someone might be able to do if they won't get up off the couch. I encourage parents to assume their children can do anything until they have good reason to believe they cannot. I think it is disrespectful to the child to do otherwise.

Sorting Out Can't Do and Won't Do

> I encourage parents to assume their children can do anything until they have good reason to believe they cannot.

I like chocolate. I especially like those chocolate bars that are made in Pennsylvania and come in dark brown wrappers. The ones with almonds are especially good. Now, suppose you told me you would give me one of those chocolate bars with almonds if I would just do something for you. I would be very interested. After all, I like chocolate. Then you tell me you will give me the chocolate bar if I will just do five hundred pushups. Do you think I am still interested? Nope. I can't do five hundred pushups. Does this mean I do not like chocolate? Nope. It means the exchange rate is out of whack. The reward is not worth the amount of work you are asking me for. But, if you told me I could have the chocolate if I did five pushups, I would start to get interested again. I can do five pushups. (Okay, maybe two pushups, but you get the point.)

Now, instead of a chocolate bar, suppose you told me you had a certified check for $10,000, and you would give it to me if

I do five hundred pushups. I still do not think I could do it, but I would give it one heck of a good try. You would find out quickly how many pushups I was capable of doing. I might even do a lot more than I thought I was capable of if that check were dangled in front of me. I do not mean to suggest that you need to offer large sums of money to your children, but I am suggesting you consider whether it is likely to seem worth it to them to do what you ask.

Some things we ask our children to do are easy for them, and it does not take much to get them to do it. Other things we ask are harder, and it may not seem worth the effort to them for whatever reason. They may lack confidence or experience. They may have tried before and failed. They may worry that they will look dumb or foolish if they do not succeed. They may just not feel like doing it. At these times, we have to find more powerful ways to encourage them to try. In other words, we have to deal with the "won't do" before we can deal with the "can't do." And the only way we can find out what they are capable of doing is by getting them to do it. Getting people to make a good effort is a question of motivation. Which brings us to the next topic.

FOUR

First the Broccoli, Then the Ice Cream

T he Really Useful Principle of Behavior #2 says that behavior is motivated. That is, behavior serves a purpose, either getting something you want or getting out of something you do not want. It turns out that it's not only *whether* you get what you want or not that matters, but also *when*.

The basic rule for motivating behavior is this: *First the Broccoli, Then the Ice Cream.* In other words, do what you are supposed to do, then you can do what you want to do. This seems like a really basic idea. Yet lots of parents seem to be surprised when they are not able to get their kids to follow even simple instructions.

"I do everything for him, he gets whatever he wants" they tell me, "and he still won't do anything for me." This is about the biggest misunderstanding of how motivation works I could imagine. But it happens all the time. Expecting children to do what they are supposed to do out of gratitude is not very realistic. Somehow, the broccoli just doesn't look as appetizing after they have already had their ice cream.

First the Ice Cream?

Suppose you worked for a company that offered this deal: We will stop by your house once a month and drop off your paycheck. We would really appreciate it if you would come to work, but you do not have to. We will drop off a paycheck for you every month, whether you come to work or not. How long do you think you would keep going to work? Some people might show up for a day or two, maybe even a week or more. But, soon enough, most people would start to find something else to do with their time. As long as the paycheck keeps coming, why go to work? Kids who get to keep all of their privileges no matter how they behave are getting the same deal. They are getting paid, but they do not have to show up for work. So they don't. Why would we expect anything different?

> In other words, do what you are supposed to do, then you can do what you want to do.

For children who have a toy room, a closet full of name-brand clothes, a television, a computer with high-speed Internet and a video game system in their room (but no fax machine, we wouldn't want to spoil them!), it can be very difficult to find ways to motivate them. If they already have free access to all this stuff, what do we have to offer? When they get into trouble and they are sent to their room, it is more like a vacation than discipline.

Now, I do not mean to suggest that children should not have toys or other amusements (I am not fully convinced that video games are ever a good idea, but that is a topic for another time.). But do they really need to have access to all their toys all the time? If they do, what do they have to work for?

Now let's think about the other side of the picture. Suppose you still work for the same company as before, but now the situation has changed. Business has been tough and money is tight. Here is the new deal: We expect you to come to work, but we are not sure we will be able to pay you. We might be able to get you a paycheck sometime, but we are not sure when. Anyway, you should just do your job because it's your responsibility, not because you get paid.

Are you going to work the next day? How about the day after that? How long would you keep showing up when there was no payoff for your efforts? When children do what we ask, day after day, but get little recognition or reward for doing it, this is the situation we put them in. They keep showing up for work, but they don't get paid. They keep eating their broccoli, but never get to taste the ice cream. It's not too surprising if they decide to stop working so hard at some point.

Some parents object to the idea of rewarding kids for doing well. Often they will say something like, "I don't think kids should have to be rewarded for things they are *supposed to do.*" What if we took the same attitude about our own jobs? Most people expect to get paid if they go to work and do their job adequately. They do not think they should have to do anything extra or spectacular, just show up, put in their time, and do what they are supposed to do. In fact, if they work extra hours or do something spectacular for the company, they expect a bonus or a raise. Why should it be different for kids? Why shouldn't they be recognized for doing what they should be doing?

It's not necessary always to reward them with money or toys or even treats. Often, children are more interested in attention, praise and recognition than anything else. Whom do you know who would like to get less recognition from their boss, teacher, or spouse? How many of us are just hoping someone will notice our good work *less*? Who among us is just sick and tired of always being told what we are doing right? Who hates just hates hearing, "Good job! Thanks"?

Your children are getting information about how to behave from somewhere or someone. If you want your voice to be heard above the noise, you should plan to let them hear from you often, and not just when they are doing something wrong. In fact, if most of your comments to your children focus on what they are doing wrong, they will learn to tune you out. Don't miss opportunities to tell them what they are doing right.

FOCUS ON THE PRESENT

I want to mention one other very important point here. If I don't show up for work one day, no one asks me to give back the money I earned the day before. I just don't earn anything that day. Most children, but especially younger kids, operate with two basic time frames: (1) now and (2) not now. One time frame matters, one does not.

A really important aspect of effective parenting is that you learn to deal with today's behavior today. This means you focus on the issues in front of you at the time. This means you do not remind the child about all the other times the same issues may have come up in the past or warn them about what life will be like in the future if they don't change their ways. This means you stay away from consequences that last days, weeks or months. Do not ask young children to work at something for two or three weeks to earn a reward. Do not take away privileges for weeks or months at a time.

There also are problems with using long-term consequences with older children or adolescents. Parents (including me) tend to forget how long they said the consequence was going to last ("Did we say he was grounded for two weeks or three? And what day was it when we said that, anyway?").

Parents often find it difficult to enforce long-term consequences because of all the other commitments the child and the family have. They end up letting the child off the hook early because of basketball practice or Tae-kwon-do or confirmation class. Sometimes parents just plain forget. When any of this happens, it mostly just makes the parent look ineffective and inconsistent to the child. This is not an image we want to promote. Also, long-term consequences tend to punish the whole family. If one child is grounded, the other kids may not get to go anywhere either.

> A really important aspect of effective parenting is that you learn to deal with today's behavior today.

Of course, not every parent lets their child off the hook early. The other possibility is that the parent is very determined and more organized than most and enforces the consequence for the full time. If the punishment lasts too long, the most likely results are (1) the child gets sneakier and learns how to avoid detection better or (2) the child resents the parent more, or both.

Here is another way to look at it. Think back to our discussion about the importance of repetition in learning. Suppose you wanted to teach your daughter how to hit a baseball. You get a bat, ball and glove together, load up the car and go to the park. You set your daughter up at home plate, show her how to stand and hold the bat properly, then walk out to the pitcher's mound. You tell her to keep her eye on the ball. You throw one pitch. She swings and misses. You say, "Nice try. We will come back in two weeks and do it again."

> You will not teach twice as big a lesson by punishing twice as long.

Does this seem like a good way to teach? Probably not. This is basically what is going on when you impose long-term consequences. You get one teaching opportunity in two weeks instead of five or fifteen or fifty or more repetitions. You will not teach twice as big a lesson by punishing twice as long. It is better to teach what you can today and move on to tomorrow. Teaching happens best in small bites delivered in a consistent way. Deal with today's behavior today.

PUNISHMENT

Any effective approach to discipline and motivation requires the use of punishment. But punishment by itself is not enough to make discipline truly effective in the long run. Without getting into a lot of boring and tedious psychology talk, let me just point out that punishment always leads to a *decrease* in some behavior. If we want a child to do less of something, punishment is a reasonable choice. However, punishment does not teach new and appropriate behavior. You can punish someone into doing *less* bad behavior, but you cannot punish them into doing *more* good behavior. Punishment is necessary, but not sufficient for good discipline.

Picture a map of the United States. Imagine you were stuck in some out-of-the-way, backwater place like Nebraska (it's right in the middle). Now suppose you called me up and asked me to give you directions for how to get from Nebraska to California. What if I told you, "Don't go to Minnesota. Don't go to Texas. Don't go to New York. Don't go to Alabama. Don't go to North Dakota, Michigan, Canada or Australia." This is not the best way to give directions, right?

> You can punish someone into doing less bad behavior, but you cannot punish them into doing more good behavior.

Yet this is essentially what punishment does. It tells your children what not to do, where not to go. When you punish, you are telling your children: "Whatever you just did, don't do that again." When someone is going the wrong way or doing something wrong, of course we want to stop them, but there needs to be more. For one thing, telling a child everything they should not do would be a really big job. The list is very long. We also want to show them the right way to go, teach them the right things to do. This is effective discipline. Punishment is only a part. It's often necessary, but never enough.

One of the big problems with punishment is that it works, but only temporarily. Imagine a mom who catches a child trying to sneak a cookie out of the cookie jar. She gives his hand a little tap and says, "No cookies." The child pulls his hand back and leaves the cookie jar alone for the moment. This punishment thing seems to work fairly well. But he still wants a cookie.

Before long, mom gets distracted and the boy is sneaking back to the cookie jar to try again. Mom spots him again. "What did I say about cookies?" she says. She remembers that giving his hand a little tap worked before because he left the cookies alone. But it did not work as well as she would like, because he came back. Maybe a little harder tap would do the trick. She slaps the back of his hand more firmly, and he leaves the cookies alone again for a time. But he still wants a cookie.

> One of the big problems with punishment is that it works, but only temporarily.

You get the idea. Unless mom gives the child a different way to earn a cookie, he probably will be back at the cookie jar again at some point. And she probably will continue to crank the punishment up a notch or two each time. "You are not listening to me. Now you will never get a cookie!" But he still wants a cookie. This is how the downward spiral of punishment happens. She keeps telling him what not to do, but does not tell him what to do instead to get what he wants. He stops for a time, but comes back and the punishment gets a little more harsh each time.

There are some other problems with relying too much or exclusively on punishment. If a child sees parents mainly as a source of punishment, the child may figure out the best way to avoid the punishment is to avoid the parent. Just being around the parent feels like punishment because all of their interactions involve negativity and criticism. Who enjoys being around people who are negative, punishing and critical of them? Obviously, it is difficult to teach someone effectively if their main goal is to avoid you. This is a damaged relationship.

Some children react to excessive punishment in a more emotional way. They may become irritable, angry and aggressive. Since nothing they do seems to be good enough to keep them from being punished, they come to believe they have no ability to control their life. They may lose confidence and become anxious, withdrawn or depressed.

Some children simply stop doing much at all under these conditions. If it seems to them that they are punished no matter what they do, they eventually give up on trying to do much of anything. Why should they try if they are only going to be punished no matter what? A number of children I have worked with have told me that they have stopped trying to do anything good or positive because they get no recognition or credit (or privileges) when they do.

Think back to our discussion about contrast. We talked about the importance of children being able to tell what behaviors will work for them by how their parents react and from what happens to them. If they are punished no matter what, or if they are never punished, there is no contrast, and learning is very difficult. Punishment is necessary for good discipline, but relying too much on punishment almost always results in resentment and emotional damage. Should you punish? Yes. But effective discipline balances positive motivation and punishment to create the greatest possible contrast and the clearest and most obvious choice for the child.

DISCIPLINE

The purpose and core of effective discipline is to *train* positive, productive and adaptive behavior, not just to punish inappropriate behavior. Successful punishment tells a child what not to do. The next thing we want to tell them is what to do instead, and then reinforce them in some way for doing it. Successful discipline is sort of like the bumpers in the gutters at the bowling alley. They keep you from getting completely off track, then nudge you back in the right direction.

Some parents I meet have gotten to be fairly good at punishment (sometimes too good), but somehow the kids still do not seem to get the point. Many of these parents have not included the "earn your privileges back" step in their discipline. Or they have fallen into the trap of extending the punishment for excessive periods of time. In fact, it is fairly common for parents to come into my office and tell me they do not know what to do with their child. They have taken everything away for weeks at a time, but the child still will not do what they are supposed to. If the child has no clear idea what has to be done to earn the stuff back, this stalemate probably will go on for a long time. Now the parents are backed into a corner. They have nothing left to work with because they have taken everything. The child thinks, "What else can they do to me if I don't listen?" There is not much learning going on here, and most of what is being learned is not helpful or productive.

Sometimes parents think they can teach a much bigger lesson by imposing a much longer or harsher punishment. This is the "home run" approach to discipline—trying to teach everything in one shot. Unfortunately, learning rarely works that way. It's a little like trying to walk your dog all at once instead of a little every day. Children who are continually grounded or confined to their rooms may not misbehave much, mainly because they do not really have the chance. The parent believes something has been accomplished because the problem behavior slows down. But as soon as the kids get another chance at the cookie jar, they take it. They are not misbehaving much while they are restricted, but they also don't have much chance to learn more positive, productive behaviors if they don't get out of their room to practice them. You can't learn something by not doing it.

You might think of problem behavior as a stone rolling downhill, picking up a little more speed each time the problem behavior happens. Punishing the behavior is like putting a barrier in front of the stone. The behavior stops, but as soon as the barrier is taken away, it may very well start to roll again unless something is done to change the momentum. Requiring the child to demonstrate an appropriate behavior to earn back privileges turns the momentum in the other direction and creates an opportunity for the parent to respond to the child in a positive way. Effective discipline most often *includes* a punishment, but it *concludes* only when the child has done something productive to earn back privileges.

We are now ready to move away from just talking about the principles behind Deliberate Discipline and to start working on specific ways to put them into action. The six steps outlined in the next section should help you stop the downhill momentum in your children's behavior and begin to turn it around.

FIVE

Six Simple (But Not Always Easy) Steps to Deliberate Discipline

F inally. We can now move forward with starting to use all of this information about behavior (our own and our kids'), learning and motivation to help build a plan and put it into action. Of course, parenting cannot easily be boiled down to just six simple steps, but the methods outlined here should provide a good starting point as well as a solid framework. These are the building blocks of Deliberate Discipline that establish the foundation for effective parenting and equip your children for a successful transition to adulthood.

If you work to make sure daily activities in your home are built around structure and regular routines, if you are clear with yourself and your children about what you expect from them, and if you have a workable and consistent approach to discipline and motivation, the job of parenting is likely to be much easier and much more successful and your children are likely to be more emotionally and behaviorally balanced. You will probably sleep a little better as well.

This section discusses general concepts and guidelines for successful motivation and discipline. Specific tools and systems will be outlined in more detail in the following chapters. The steps are not in a particular order, though obviously some steps have to happen before others. Some things can be done today; others may take several days, weeks or months to put in place completely. Some you may still be working on the day your child leaves for college or moves out of the house for good.

Naturally, it is best if anyone who interacts regularly with the child (mom, dad, stepparents, grandparents) have an active role in building the plan and putting it into action. Almost always, one person takes more responsibility for working with the children, but it is obviously important that everyone have a similar understanding of the goals and methods. This is particularly true when it comes to setting up expectations and deciding how discipline will be handled. If the adults are not all informed and in agreement, they probably will not deal with behavior in the same way. No repetition. No learning. Little success.

STEP 1: ACT LIKE A GROWN-UP (PART 2)

Way back in chapter 1, we talked about how important it is for your children to see you as somehow different from them. The best way to accomplish this, of course, is to actually be different in how you look, think, talk and act toward your children. We have talked about a lot of these issues in the previous pages, but one thing we haven't discussed is how important it is to your children that you pay attention to your own life and your adult relationships.

Do a quick inventory. If most of your calorie intake comes from eating crusts and leftovers off your kids' plates, if more than half your clothes have a jelly stain on them somewhere and 90 percent of the mileage on your car is put on driving kids to a school, music lessons or sports activities, you probably need to make some changes. If the most stimulating intellectual exercise you get is trying to figure out what the mysterious object you found under your kid's bed might be, some adjustments are in order.

Taking care of and training your children is an important job, but you are not likely to do it well if parenting is your only focus. If you want to succeed as a parent, plan to invest some time, effort and energy in nurturing your own adult activities, interests and relationships. In his remarkable book, *The Last Lecture*, Randy Pausch said it this way: "The best piece of parenting advice I've ever heard is from flight attendants. If things get really tough, grab your own oxygen mask first." In other words, it is hard to be truly useful to your children or anyone else if you are worn out physically, emotionally or otherwise. You must continue to recharge your own batteries if you expect to have the energy you need to jump start your children's lives.

This means that if you are married, you continue to invest in and nurture your relationship with your spouse, and you spend time doing and talking about issues that don't always center on the kids. Obviously, you do need to discuss important issues about your children, but if this is your only topic of shared interest, you may want to rethink your activities. If you regularly spend all of your time and energy on your children, they will come to expect that this is how their lives should be and will react strongly (and most likely negatively) when you want time for yourself or when someone else (like a teacher, coach or spouse) expects them to manage on their own. The sooner they get used to the idea they are not at the center of your universe, the better.

Single Parents

If you are single with children, it is important to develop interests, activities and relationships outside your home with other actual grown-up people. I realize that, for many single parents, this is easier said than done. It is difficult enough for two parents to accomplish this, much less for single parents. By the time you take care of your home, finances, job, car, cooking and supervise school work and chores, there usually is a lot more day left at the end of the energy than energy at the end of the day (not to mention too much month left at the end of the money).

Nonetheless, it is truly important that you pay attention to your own life too. It is way too easy to lose your adult perspective if most or all your interactions are with kids. Maybe it is as simple as allowing yourself a little time to read something other than books about parenting, take a class at the community college or church, watch a grown-up television show (if there is such a thing), or talk to a friend over a cup of coffee or on the phone.

When it comes to relations with the opposite sex, though, considerable caution is in order. If you are single, be careful about moving too quickly to include your children in your developing relationships. In general, waiting longer is almost always better, especially in the early stages after a separation, divorce or death of a spouse. Children who have lost a parent by whatever means are likely to be very vulnerable and to feel as if circumstances are being imposed on them against their will. To them, being obligated to participate in a new relationship may feel like just another example of how little control they have over their own lives. This can have the effect of adding another level of uncertainty at a time when they are already feeling insecure.

If you allow your new "friend" to come to your home or participate in family activities too soon, your children learn to associate them with uncomfortable emotions. They will most likely react in one of two ways: (1) they will become too quickly and too tightly attached and feel the loss very deeply if the relationship does not work out, or (2) they will resent the other person for trying to take the place of the missing parent and act out behaviorally or try to assert themselves too strongly.

I have had the unfortunate opportunity to observe firsthand how forcing a new relationship of this kind can damage families. It is almost always better to wait at least a year before beginning to pursue new relationships, then to keep these relationships separate, and to introduce the new person only very slowly. Begin by choosing shared activities that will be enjoyable to the children, that do not make great demands on them, and that take place in the community, rather than in your home. If your children learn to associate the new person with positive experiences and emotions over a period of time, you will improve the chances for long-term relationship success.

STEP 2: MAKE ROUTINES HAPPEN ROUTINELY

It should be abundantly clear by now that structure and predictability are a big deal for kids. If you doubt this, just pay attention for a few days. Notice how many times your children ask a question about when something will happen, where you are going, what happens next, who will be there and so on. Notice how they react when you do something completely different from what you said you were going to do.

Just like us, kids feel more comfortable when they know what is going on. It seems simple, but few things contribute more to behavioral and emotional stability in children. And it's not just kids.

If you don't think routine is important to you as an adult, try sleeping on the other side of the bed, crossing your legs with the other leg on top, putting your billfold in a different pocket or driving a different route to work or school each day. Think about how it felt when you started a new job or moved to a different neighborhood or city. A lot of your time, effort and energy goes into just trying to figure out where everything is located, how long it takes to get there and what you need to do next. Helping your kids develop good habits now will save everybody a lot of time later. You won't waste time looking for your keys in the morning if you put them in the same place every night. The same thing goes for the kids' book bags or high school ID tag.

We talked earlier about the importance of repetition to learning. Routines and habits are the bricks and mortar of repetition. The more consistent your children's regular activities become, the more time and energy they (and you) can devote to other, more enjoyable and rewarding activities. The more time you spend looking for the car keys or the book bags, the less time you have to enjoy the rest of the day, and the more stressed you will be.

Think about what it was like when you were trying to learn to drive a car or to play a musical instrument. When you were first learning, everything took a lot of time, effort and concentration, but, as you kept practicing, even these complicated and demanding skills became more and more "automatic" and less effortful. If each step is well learned, the whole process is well learned. If you help your children learn to put their dishes in the sink after dinner every night, start on homework as soon as they get home each day and always brush their teeth right after they put on their pajamas, these habits will become ingrained and automatic, just like your basic driving skills. In general, life is easier if you figure out the best way to take care of routine requirements, then keep doing it that way.

Helping kids learn how to keep some order in their lives can be challenging. Let's face it, keeping order in our own lives can be tough. In many families, both parents work, sometimes on different schedules. Kids tend to have a lot of commitments of their own. I know kids who have some sport, music lesson or other activity every week night and most weekends.

At some point, whatever benefit there may be for them in being involved in all this stuff is offset by the unsettled feelings that happen when there seems to be no rhythm or regularity in their lives. If you leave the decision about what they will be involved in up to your kids, you can count on doing a lot of driving and probably having to deal with unsettled, anxious kids at some point.

For most kids, *everything* sounds interesting, and they will want to try it all even if there are not enough hours in the day to fit it all in. This is an area where the adults need to impose some control. I encourage parents to consider limiting their children to no more than one sport and one other activity (play group, music lessons, scouts) at a time. It is important that home feel like a safe harbor for your children, a place to slow down, settle in and rest a bit, not just somewhere to eat and change clothes on the way to the next activity.

Structure and routines are really important, but there is a difference between a structured environment and a rigid one. In fact, in the midst of all the scheduled and structured activity, you want to be sure you make room for some unstructured time for them to just play and be a kid. Structure is truly necessary, but be sure you don't eliminate all of the opportunities to relax and recuperate.

We will take a look at three ways to build more structure into your children's daily lives: schedules, procedures and traditions.

> In fact, in the midst of all the scheduled and structured activity, you want to be sure you make room for some unstructured time for them to just play and be a kid.

Do a quick inventory. Think for a moment about how things go in your home now. If I took each member of your family aside one at a time and asked about their daily life, would everyone know and agree about when and how various activities happen? Would the children all be able to tell me procedures for handling routine tasks like hygiene, homework and housekeeping? Could they tell me what they will be doing right after school or before bed?

Most homes with children feel chaotic at times, but your efforts always should be in the direction of trying to minimize this by making events, activities and schedules predictable. If day-to-day life *always* feels chaotic around your home, you may want to spend a little extra time on this section before moving on.

Schedules

Schedules represent the *when* of family routines. It is hard to exaggerate the importance of maintaining daily and weekly schedules, especially for younger children, but also even for adolescents who are learning how to manage more demands on their own time. When you have reliable schedules for events such as bedtime, wake time and meal times, each day will seem to have rhythm and continuity. It will feel more comfortable.

Anyone who has taken a sleep deprived or hungry toddler shopping can testify to the effect a lack of sleep (or food) has on behavior. Other inconsistencies in schedules can be just as disruptive, though you may not see the results quite as quickly.

It is important to try to be aware not only of *when* things happen, but also *how long* they are happening. It is much easier to allow television, video games and other meaningless activities to creep in on your children's lives if you do not have set time limits for them. If everyone knows the television does not get turned on until after dinner and gets turned off at 8:00 every night, there will be less negative reaction when it happens. If the time changes every night, your kids will be a lot more likely to try to negotiate or argue for just one more program or a few more minutes of viewing time. If everything is open to negotiation, you probably will end up raising a house full of junior lawyers.

For younger children, who have only a vague idea of how to keep track of time, focus on the sequence of activities rather than on the specific times. Try to keep the same order from one time to the next. Review what you have already done and preview what you will be doing next to keep them oriented to where they are in the process. "Okay, everybody has their pajamas on. Let's go get our teeth brushed, and then we will be ready to read a story." Your home does not need to run like a military camp, but routine events should happen, well, routinely.

Time Together: It is often said that the greatest gift you can give is your time because it is the one thing no one can get more of. Scheduling time and activities *with* your children (not just *for* them) delivers a powerful message that you value them enough to give them some of your most precious resource. If you do not make these times a priority, chances are good that some other less valuable activities will fill the vacuum in your time and theirs.

> For younger children, who have only a vague idea of how to keep track of time, focus on the sequence of activities rather than on the specific times.

Regular shared meal times provide an important time for the family to reconnect. This includes the time involved in preparing meals and cleaning up afterward as well. If the most reliable feature of meals at your house is that they come wrapped in paper or cardboard boxes, you are missing out on a valuable opportunity. Times set aside on a regular basis for homework and chore completion reinforce the importance of taking care of routine responsibilities, particularly if the *First the Broccoli* (chores and homework), *Then the Ice Cream* (play time) approach is followed.

Scheduled times for family meetings and family fun nights communicate the message that time together is important and that parents value their interactions with the children. These times provide a chance for children to be heard and to better understand their place within the family structure. These times also provide opportunities for parents to express their own ideas and values to the children outside the framework of a disciplinary interaction.

A lot of people I know maintain a calendar that lists all of the appointments and other important responsibilities for their family. If your calendar is full most days, it may be useful to mark down appointments for even more important events like family game night and to treat these the way you would other important obligations. You demonstrate how important these times are by making them a priority and turning down any other activities that would interfere. For many families (including mine), if it does not get scheduled, it does not happen.

Time Apart: Sharing time, events and activities with your children on a regular basis is invaluable. At the same time, it is important that children learn that adults are not responsible for entertaining them all day every day. Scheduling *some* time with them does not mean you schedule *all* your time with them. Encouraging independent play skills and helping children develop an ability to keep themselves occupied without your involvement are also important goals. If you are reliable in spending time with your children when you say you will, they are much more likely to be willing to wait and entertain themselves for a time when you are not available.

By the time they are three or four years old, children should be able to play independently away from you for fifteen to thirty minutes or more. They should have enough confidence that you will be where you are supposed to be that they feel comfortable exploring a little on their own. They should be certain that, if they really need you for something, you will be there to help. They should be equally sure that, if they interrupt you for no good reason, you will tell them to leave you alone and "go play" until you decide you are ready for them.

When children are playing on their own, it is best if you check on them rather than waiting for them to come to you. This helps maintain your "grown-up" presence. It lets them know you are still there and aware of them even when you are not in the same room, which makes them feel more secure. It also gives you a chance to see what they are up to. If you wait until they have to seek you out, they are more likely to be acting out of insecurity and to feel as if they have to take responsibility for making sure you are still there. If you gradually increase the amount of time you are away, they will learn to feel comfortable being on their own for long periods.

Obviously, caring for infants and toddlers takes a lot of time and attention. They require close and consistent supervision. In fact, continuing to monitor and supervise whereabouts, activities and associates is important all the way through the high school years. One of the best predictors of how much trouble a child or adolescent gets into is how much unsupervised time they have.

But supervision does not mean keeping them within eyeshot at every moment, it means staying aware of where they are and what they are up to. Train them early on to be independently functional and reliable, but to know you are paying attention and this process gets easier. Trust, but check.

Procedures

This is the "how" part of family routines. Procedures would include such items as where to put our shoes and coats when we come in the house, steps for bedtime routine, how to be excused from the table, how to get parents' attention, how to ask permission and so on. As children mature, more complicated procedures like how to conduct yourself in public, how to disagree appropriately, and how to manage curfew can be taught. The more consistent these procedures are, the easier they are to learn, remember and repeat. The better they are learned, the less effort they take and the less chance there is for conflict about them.

> Practice does not make perfect at all. Practice makes whatever you practice.

Just about everyone has heard the saying, "Practice makes perfect." Unfortunately, this is really not true. Practice does not make perfect at all. Practice makes whatever you practice. When kids or families practice doing something in an inconsistent and disorganized way, they will continue to do it in an inconsistent and disorganized way. But, for most children, if you let them know how you want something done, train them to do it, and then let them know how much you appreciate it when it is done right, there is a very good chance that life will get better for everyone.

Some simple procedures can be taught all in one shot. Putting your dirty socks in the hamper or putting the forks next to the plates on the dinner table are basically one-step operations. As the tasks get more complicated, we may be able to train only some part of the process. Often, the best way to train is to let children do as much of the task as they can before we step in and train the next step. At other times, we might do the first few steps and let them finish the job. We put the plates, glasses and napkins on the table, and they put on the silverware. After they have done this successfully a few times, they get to put on the napkins and the silverware, then the plates, napkins and silverware and so on.

There is much more being learned here than just how to set a table. More general skills like how to break down a complicated task into smaller, easier to manage pieces and how to cooperate with someone else are also being learned, and kids get to see that skills improve over time if they stick with it.

Procedures for discipline should be at the top of the list of routines that are well understood by everyone. The details will change somewhat depending on the age or developmental level of the child, but the basic ideas of contrast and repetition will not. (You will learn more about specific disciplinary procedures in later chapters.)

From the beginning, your children should learn they will get attention, privileges and rewards when they are behaving well and almost nothing when they are not. But they also should understand that being disciplined is a temporary condition and that they are active participants in disciplinary events, not passive recipients. Discipline does not just happen to them. They are directly involved in the process and in determining the outcome. They should learn that you will stop them promptly when they are headed the wrong way, teach them what to do instead and give them a chance to get back on track. They should know from experience that punishment will be delivered reliably and that it will be painful, but never harmful. They should also know that when rewards or privileges are earned, parents can be counted on to deliver them just as reliably and consistently.

Traditions

Family traditions can be an important part of connecting a child to the immediate family, to the extended family and to previous and future generations of the family and community. Schedules and procedures build structure and continuity in the short term, traditions give kids a sense of longer term stability. You might think of traditions as the "punctuation" in the daily flow of life. They provide a chance to pause for a moment, rather than just being swept along in the river of day-to-day activities.

Traditions can be built around all kinds of things. Major events like birthdays and holidays and milestones like weddings and graduations are obvious examples. But traditions might also include more basic and frequent events such as family game night or movie night once a week. Family vacations or regular family outings can provide a touchstone for measuring the family's life together. Eating particular foods and dressing and decorating in a particular way for holidays and events all contribute to the special feel of traditional events.

Annual traditions remind children of their own importance in family history and of the continuity of the family unit. These events also provide an opportunity to reflect on what has occurred for the family and for individual family members since the last such event. Being reminded of family history and culture provides an anchor point and a sense of place.

When these traditional events are planned, they must be considered a priority, especially for the parents. Other activities and requirements should take a back seat to these commitments. If you often find reasons not to participate in planned traditional activities, your children will say they understand, but what they will understand most is what your behavior says—that you have something better to do and that other items on your agenda are more important to you than they are.

When Families Separate: One of the main causes of problems for children of divorced or separated parents is the disruption of their routines and traditions. For children in this situation, their sense of security already has been shaken. They have experienced the loss of the foundational relationship and the core structure of their family when their parents separated. Then, this upset is multiplied and amplified by changes and inconsistency in their routines and habits. They stay at different places during the week. Schedules and procedures vary from house to house. They have to put effort into keeping track of clothes, toys and school materials in a way they did not before. They sleep in different beds and associate with different playmates. They go from seeing some family members every day to seeing them every other weekend or whenever it happens to work out. They lose the continuity of holidays because their time is divided between homes.

All too often, children in separated or divorced families are exposed to the adults' own struggles and uncertainties and to too much information about legal, financial and personal matters. They may hear negative comments from one or both parents about the other, further shaking their trust and confidence in their parents and all adults. Since the parents' feelings for each other seem to have changed dramatically, the children may wonder whether their parents will stop loving them too.

Children should not be used as messengers, especially not to tell the other parent that he or she is doing something wrong ("Tell your dad the child support payment is late."). They should not be asked to spy on the other parent's personal and financial affairs or asked to choose sides. Doing any of this will almost certainly result in damaging the child's relationship with *both* parents in the end. Children should not be instructed on how they should behave at the other parent's home or made to feel they are somehow disloyal if they enjoy their visits with the other parent.

Children have little choice or control over when or how visits happen and must be allowed to do what they think necessary to fit in at either home. It is especially important that children not be relied upon to help their parents emotionally through this difficult time.

Separation and divorce are almost always emotionally charged and troubling events for the adults as well as for the children. Often, the time before the separation has been difficult and the family structure already has broken down. It is easy for parents to be distracted from the needs of the children during this time as they work through their own emotional issues and all the practical details and logistics. Children do best in this difficult situation when change is kept to a minimum.

In general, if someone is going to be inconvenienced as a result of separation or divorce, it should be the parents, not the children. Every effort should be made to keep them in the same home, school and church. Their activities and friendships should not be disrupted. Schedules and routines should look as much alike as possible from one home to the other. Expectations for their behavior and disciplinary and motivational methods should be similar.

Parents who are separated or divorced tell me often about how much more difficult things are for their children when they come back from a visit with the other parent. As often as not, these problems are largely the result of different expectations, schedules and routines in the two homes. Different bedtimes, mealtimes, changes in activities and differences in overall expectations cause more problems for the children than anyone else. If there is no other area where separated parents can agree or cooperate, working together for the benefit of the children should be the one. Sadly, this often is not the case. For those parents who are able to agree, doing their best to keep everything they can as stable and consistent as possible for the children should be a priority.

STEP 3: FIGURE OUT WHAT YOU WANT

It is hard to know if your expectations are being met if neither you nor your kids know what it is you expect. This seems pretty obvious. Yet every so often I can count on seeing parents and children who have been arguing for months or years over the same issue: what the kids are supposed to be doing. How does this happen?

- Sometimes the children have learned to "forget" expectations because it is convenient for them to do so. If parents' only reaction to these lapses is to complain or lecture, the kids' memories continue to be fuzzy.

- Sometimes parents are inconsistent in what they expect from one day to the next, and the children have a hard time figuring out what the rules of the day might be.

- Sometimes the expectations are unreasonable or excessive and the kids realize there is no way for them to measure up, so they just try to stay out of the way.

- Sometimes expectations just have not been communicated clearly.

I have had any number of parents tell me they are sure their kids know exactly what is expected of them, only to find out later from the kids that they truly have no idea. Sometimes, the children think they already are doing what the parent wants and are confused about why they are still getting in trouble.

> It is hard to know if your expectations are being met if neither you nor your kids know what it is you expect.

In any case, it is hard to know if you are getting anywhere if no one has any idea where you are supposed to be going. It is important that you be clear and realistic in your expectations for your children, but also with your expectations for yourself and for the process of parenting.

Expectations for the Process

Few things in life are learned in one shot. Sure, putting your hand on a hot stove one time convinces most people not to do that again, but there are exceptions even to this. Insulting someone who is three times your size might result in one-shot learning as well, but most learning happens more gradually and incrementally. Some complex skills take years or decades to learn. Some of what we want our children to learn can be taught fairly quickly, but more complicated things like social skills or regulating emotions can take much, much longer and require a more intensive and persistent effort.

It is important always to keep in mind that parenting is a process, not a one-time event. Remember, getting your kids from here to adulthood happens step by step by step. You can't do it overnight.

I encourage parents to think of the process of parenting as being something like shaping a pot on a potter's wheel. You start off with a shapeless mass of clay and an idea of what you hope the finished product will look like. If you try to squeeze it into shape all at once, you don't get a pot, you get clay all over yourself and the walls. You get a mess.

Most learning, but especially learning complicated skills or concepts, happens gradually over time. Trying to force kids into a particular behavioral shape all at once usually produces an unpleasant and messy result, and you never get to where you hoped to be. At the same time, you should keep in mind that parenting is

> It is important always to keep in mind that parenting is a process, not a one-time event.

an *active* process. If you don't keep steady pressure on, the pot doesn't look any more like a pot from one day to the next. You should not expect to get huge amounts of teaching out of any one experience, but get what training you can, shape the pot just a little bit more and move on. Repetition. Repetition. Repetition.

Expectations for Yourself

Parents sometimes tell me they are really worried that they are going to do something wrong in raising their children. Working with parents and children is an often uncertain business, but one thing I can guarantee is that you definitely *will* do some things wrong, probably a lot of things. But, it's okay. Kids are really quite resilient, and, if you accept the fact that learning happens bit by bit through repetition, you realize you only have to get it right *most* of the time for your kids to get the message. Of course, it will take a whole lot longer to get the point across if you are inconsistent over a long period of time, but you are not going to ruin them by goofing up once in a while. I could fill another book with all of the mistakes I made as a parent. This is not permission to be sloppy; it is just permission to take it easy on yourself when you mess up.

One other thing to keep in mind here is that normal kids misbehave. Some normal kids misbehave a lot. Your responsibility is to do the best you can as consistently as you can and to recognize that sometimes children choose to do the "wrong thing" and accept the consequences. This is a valid choice. You do not have to jump in to fix every problem. Misbehavior by children is not a sign of parental failure; it is just an indicator for what you need to be working on. Just follow what you know about behavior and learning and let the process develop as long as there is no real threat of damage or harm. Just because they don't get it right right away does not mean you are doing something wrong. Remember, parenting is a process. Even if the pot gets a little uneven and wobbly sometimes (and it probably will), you can usually go back and rework it.

It is also important to keep in mind that children, just like adults, have free will. Even with the best efforts of parents and others, some kids continue to make bad choices. Some behaviors are difficult to fix. Sometimes, the best you can do is not make it worse. Do the right thing as you and other adults you trust see it and chances are you will have a good outcome in the end. Try to micro manage every behavior, every day, and chances are you will make yourself and your kids crazy.

Expectations for Your Children

Parents who expect nothing from their children almost always get what they expect. Nothing. This can be frustrating for parents, but the bigger concern is the effect on the kids. Children who have few or no expectations placed on them are being robbed. They are robbed of the opportunity to enjoy success and to learn how to deal with failure. They are robbed of practice with important life skills. They are robbed of the chance to be praised for a job well done because the job isn't getting done at all. They are robbed of feeling good about their accomplishments. They are robbed of the sense that their parents trust them and have confidence in them to work on important tasks. Of course, this does not mean that children are always grateful to have expectations placed on them or enthusiastic about the work involved.

I talk often with parents about the importance of helping their children learn how to take care of routine responsibilities in a routine way. This is the fundamental and truly essential skill we are teaching when we set up clear expectations and then follow the *First the Broccoli, Then the Ice Cream* rule: Do what you are supposed to do, then you can do what you want to do.

Think about how much of your daily life consists of just doing routine things—everything from getting up, getting dressed, and getting to work or school on time each morning to paying the bills, doing the dishes, balancing the checkbook, and making sure the oil gets changed in the car. We may not want to teach an eight year old how to change the oil in the car or balance the checkbook, but we can teach them the more general skill of responsibility by developing and enforcing expectations for rules, chores and homework.

Although parents often come to me with concerns about grades, I most often recommend they not focus exclusively on grades as part of their expectations for the child. One of the problems with using grades is that grades are not always readily available. Sometimes they are issued only twice in a semester. It is difficult to monitor them day by day, and this undermines the idea of managing today's behavior today. In my experience, a majority of problems with grades result from assignments not being completed or turned in on time. This means the child is not giving regular attention to academics, so when the test rolls around, there are holes in the knowledge and skills and the grades suffer further.

> Parents who expect nothing from their children almost always get what they expect.

Most of the time, if students do homework regularly and completely, they will earn the grade they deserve. Furthermore, assignment completion is easier to monitor and easier to verify at home. I tell kids that work completion is their main responsibility and the grade is important, but secondary. They will be held accountable for completing their work, whether they get credit or not. If they are allowed to "blow off" work just because it is late and they will get reduced or no credit, this is an enticement to neglect their assignments more, and bad habits continue to build. I have had numerous clients who are required to spend the first week or two of summer vacation completing work that will get them no credit.

An important goal in setting up expectations for our children is to find a balance between asking too little and asking too much. We want to challenge them, but not overwhelm them. The idea is to provide regular experience with success in accomplishing meaningful tasks, but also to encourage them to stretch themselves and try to do a little more than they might be inclined to attempt on their own. We want them to get practice with the skills they have, but always nudge them in the direction of learning new and more difficult skills.

This means that everything will not always be done as well or as completely as parents might like. Sometimes parents have to learn how to accept a bed that is not made just right or a crumb or two left on the counter after it has been wiped down by a child. Sometimes children fail. In fact, if they are not failing once in a while, you probably are not challenging them enough. Sometimes what we ask is difficult and takes effort and they resist and challenge us. This is just the process of learning at work. They are learning to do the task, but they are also learning to deal with frustration and how to work persistently, two truly essential life skills.

Parents have told me "it's just easier" to do the job themselves rather than to battle with their children about chores and other expectations. They are right in thinking it is easier at that moment, but it is just about guaranteed to be more difficult in the long run for everyone involved. It is harder for the child who grows up without learning how to manage daily life and eventually harder for the parent who gets less and less out of the child over time.

Often, children who become accustomed to parents taking this approach learn that if they just drag their feet and complain enough, they will get out of doing whatever it is they don't want to do. The parent will end up doing it because "it's just easier." This teaches children to put more energy into avoiding responsibility and getting other people to do things for them than they put into learning important skills for themselves.

> Sometimes children fail. In fact, if they are not failing once in a while, you probably are not challenging them enough.

Part of the difficulty in coming up with a list of expectations is that behavior can be a lot different from one day to the next, and sometimes for no apparent reason. Children learn, grow and mature at different rates. What is reasonable to expect from one child at age five or nine may not be reasonable for the next five or nine year old. There are no absolute rules for setting up expectations according to age or grade level, but there are some guidelines.

I usually talk about two main areas of expectations for children: rules and chores. Usually, I think of rules as more general guidelines for behavior and chores as more specific, regularly assigned tasks that are to be completed by a particular time. What the two categories have in common is that they should be few in number, reasonable for the child's age and abilities, and clearly spelled out.

Rules: There is no "one size fits all" list of rules for all kids. Most parents have a lot of responsibilities they would *like* their kids to do, but some are less important to them than others. Generally, I ask parents to try to come up with a list of between four and six household rules. Sometimes it turns out to be a few more, but if the list gets too much longer, it is hard for kids or parents to keep track of all of them, and enforcement tends to be inconsistent. In other words, there is no repetition. Of course, we know by now what that means. It is much better to have fewer rules that are enforced all of the time than a lot of rules that are each enforced some of the time.

I suggest parents focus on what I call the "non-negotiables" when working out rules for their home. These are the items they feel they *must* have from their kids. Other things parents might *like* to have, but can live without, are usually not included on the initial list. This does not mean you stop teaching other skills, it just means they are not emphasized as much. Some items on the list might be things the child already does well most of the time. Often, it turns out that even behaviors that are not on the list improve as parents get more reliable in enforcing the requirements that *are* on the list.

If you were to have only one rule, it should be this: Follow instructions the first time they are given. You can find a way to apply this rule to just about any situation. Beyond that, the list should reflect whatever the parents are most interested in. Sometimes bad language or arguing is a big concern. Sometimes it is aggressive behavior. Sometimes getting to bed on time or keeping up with hygiene is the big issue.

Even if your children are too young to read, there is some benefit to working out a list of rules, especially if parents do it together. Parents sometimes assume they have the same expectations for the kids, but when they get down to writing them out, they find out there is more disagreement than they thought.

For adolescents, writing down expectations is even more important since they are more likely to conveniently "forget" what they were supposed to do. Writing down expectations is also a good way to remind yourself of what it is you are trying to focus on. Rules should be appropriate to the child's age or stage of development. They should be stated positively whenever possible; tell them what you want, not what you do not want. For example: "Food and drink in the kitchen only," not "No food in your bedroom."

> If you were to have only one rule, it should be this: Follow instructions the first time they are given.

Here are some ideas about rules that might be included on your list, depending on the age of the child and the particular areas of concern:

- Follow instructions the first time given.

- Use appropriate language.

- Be ready for school by 7:30 a.m.
  (dressed, fed and in the car).

- Do homework before anything else after school.
  Keep hands and feet to self.

- TV/video games/computer off by 8:30 p.m.

- In bed, lights out by 10:00 p.m.

Two Rules for Making Rules

1. Rules without consequences are just suggestions.

Several years ago, I made a trip to Louisiana. A friend and colleague of mine was getting married near her family home in Metairie. I flew into the New Orleans airport, rented a car and headed off down the highway. The sun was shining, and I had the window down enjoying the ride. A little way down the road, I noticed a few of the cars in front of me were putting on their brakes. A few moments later, I could see why. A police car was parked by the side of the highway. Soon, there were brake lights going on all over the place. I slowed down, too (not that I was speeding or anything, I was just being cautious). As I got closer and got a better look, I could see there was nobody in the car. It was just an empty police car, but it was very effective at getting me and a lot of other drivers to slow down.

The other drivers and I were all following the Really Useful Rule of Behavior #2. We all wanted to avoid something bad happening. But here's the deal: not everyone slowed down. The people who live around there see that police car out there all the time. They know there is nobody in it. Not only did they not slow down, they were honking and waving at the rest of us to get us going.

The point is this: If you have rules, but all you do is remind, lecture, complain and nag when they are broken, you are like an empty police car to your children. You may look like you should have some authority, but they will learn to ignore you unless you get out of the car and write some tickets. If you are not prepared to enforce a rule, best not to make it.

2. **Rules and consequences without a relationship is a recipe for rebellion.**

You may be able to enforce behavior for a time by relying just on consequences, maybe even a long time, but your kids will grow and mature and they will begin to spend more and more time out of your sight. They will find themselves more often in situations where they have to make a decision about how to behave without you there to help them. Fear of a negative consequence will help some, but they are more likely to make the better decision if they truly respect the purpose of your rules and do not want to disappoint you. If you squeeze too tight for too long, they will take advantage of the first chance they have to exercise a little freedom.

You want rules to be short, simple and clear enough that either parent, grandparents, babysitters or anyone else will have no trouble deciding whether or not a rule is being followed. If you have a child who tends to be stubborn, it is best not to make rigid rules about eating, sleeping, talking (or not talking), or toileting habits.

What these four things have in common is that the child has total control over whether they do them or not. You can make them sit at the table, but you can't make them eat. You can make them stay in their room, but you can't make them sleep. You can make them sit on the toilet, but you can't make them go. You can't make them talk. If you set up battles over these behaviors with a strong-willed child, you will lose most of them. The child will be reinforced for resisting and be emboldened to resist you more. You will lose authority in your child's eyes.

Chores: Most of us spend at least part of our day doing tasks we would rather not do. I am not fond of filling out insurance forms, shoveling snow or loading the dishwasher, but I do all of these behaviors from time to time. These are chores, the unpleasant necessities of life. I would be much better off and my wife and my office staff would be a lot happier with me if I were better at taking care of them more consistently.

I see a lot of children who would have a much easier time in life if they were just able to take care of their own routine responsibilities in a more consistent way. If we want to teach our children this skill, the best thing is to get them some practice and the best place to practice is at home. I would much rather parents help their kids learn important life skills, ideas and values rather than allowing teachers or someone else to do this. Also, for most kids, the privileges they care most about are at home, not at school or daycare. This means parents have more tools available with which to motivate them.

Parents also have the advantage of being able to start the process of teaching their children how to handle responsibility long before they ever see the inside of a school building. It may start with just putting their pajamas back in the drawer each morning, their dirty dishes in the sink after dinner or picking up one toy before getting out something else. Even children as young as two or three should be able to start learning how to manage some small tasks, and most kids will be eager to do so and prove how capable they are.

Keep in mind that the real skill that is being taught when children do chores is not how to vacuum or fold towels (most kids could figure out how to do these on their own). The real skill you are teaching is how to take care of routine responsibilities in a routine way.

Examples of Age-Appropriate Chores

Age 2

Pick up toys

Dust with a dust cloth/
sock on hand

Water plants

Sort clothes by color

Wipe up spills

Tear up lettuce for salad

Stir batter

Age 3 to 4

Put dirty clothes in the
hamper or basket

Put clean clothes in the
closet or drawer

Sort and fold laundry

Unpack groceries

Rinse fruits and
vegetables

Sort recyclables

Set the table with plates
and napkins

Ages 5 to 6

Make the bed

Feed and water pets

Pick up the mail

Set and clear the table (no
sharp knives)

Pour drinks into cups

Pull weeds in the garden

Help wash the dog

Collect trash from
wastebaskets

Ages 10 to 12

Mow

Shovel snow

Help wash the car

Operate the washer and
dryer

Help prepare simple
meals

Plan a meal

Wash windows

Run own bath/shower

Iron

Neighborhood jobs
(pets, lawns, paper)

Ages 7 to 9	Ages 13 to 17
Take out trash	Replace light bulbs
Rake leaves	Operate snow blower
Help with grocery shopping	All parts of laundry
Make and pack a lunch	Heavier yard work/ cleaning
Clean bathroom	Change sheets and bedding
Vacuum	
Load/unload dishwasher	Painting
Set table and clear table	Run errands
	Prepare family meal
	Beginning car maintenance (with supervision)
	Community jobs

Here are some of the kinds of tasks you might consider assigning. Keep in mind that kids grow and mature at different rates, so what is appropriate for one child at a given age might not be appropriate for your child. If you expect to have trouble getting your child to start doing more chores, do not assign tasks that *must* be done such feeding the cat or taking out the garbage. If your child decides to be stubborn and not comply, someone will have to feed the cat or it will die. Someone will have to take out the garbage or it will stink up the house. In this case, the stubborn child is rewarded for stalling (passive noncompliance), and the parent looks less effective. More details about chore lists will be discussed in a later section.

Obviously, there are any number of other items that might be on this list. In my opinion, asking children to take care of their own space and possessions (such as cleaning their rooms) is important, but from the earliest time they do chores, they also should be doing tasks that contribute to the family welfare and the household.

STEP 4: DON'T MAKE THEM FIGURE OUT WHAT YOU WANT

Once you have figured out what you want from your children, the next step is to make sure they *don't* have to figure it out because you communicate your expectations clearly.

Suppose you were driving along and saw a sign that said this:

A few minutes later, a police officer pulls you over and writes you a ticket for doing 48 miles per hour. What would you think about this? I am guessing you would not think it was fair to be punished for something when the expectation was not clearly communicated.

Children react the same way. We sometimes assume they know what they are supposed to do or that they should know. I have had parents tell me they are sure their child knows what is expected of them only to have the child tell me a few minutes later they have no idea or they have a completely different understanding. Sometimes kids tell me they have to guess what their parents want because it changes from one day to the next. Then they get punished for not doing something they were not even sure they were supposed to do. Sometimes this situation has been going on for months or years. Children think this is unfair because it *is* unfair. If we want to hold them accountable, we should at least let them know what they will be held accountable for.

Verbal Expectations

When children are younger, communicating our expectations is simpler, more direct and more immediate. We let them know what we want from them mostly by just telling them. If you think about it, you give lots of instructions to kids throughout the day. Some are small and do not matter too much like, "Sit down so I can brush your hair." Others are more important like, "Get out of the street." Whatever the instruction, it is important to communicate it clearly.

Giving clear instructions seems like a really simple idea, but a fair number of the parents who come into my office seem to have a hard time with it. A common difficulty for parents is having a tendency to turn their instructions into a question or a suggestion instead of a command. They say something like, "Honey, do you think you could pick up the toys now?" instead of a more clear and direct command such as, "Please pick up the toys."

When it comes to giving instructions, simple and short is better. If you want your child to take your instructions seriously, learn to give them once and then enforce compliance. If you are willing to give an instruction multiple times before you enforce it, you are well on your way to becoming that empty police car.

Guidelines for Giving Effective Instructions

1. **Make sure the instruction is phrased as a command, not a question or suggestion:**

    *   "Please wash your hands now." NOT: "Would you like to wash your hands now?" or "Maybe you should think about washing your hands now."

    *   Make it clear to the child that you are *telling them* what to do.

    *   It may help to train yourself to start your commands with the word *please.* Saying *please* demonstrates good manners and respect, but also prevents you from turning your command into a question because it would sound funny.

2. **Keep it short:**

    *   "Please hang up your coat." NOT: "You know your coat belongs in the closet, not on the floor. Please hang it up before someone trips over it."

    *   Anything more than seven words is a lecture.

3. **Use "start" commands, not "stop" commands; describe what you want, not what you do not want:**

   - "Please sit down." NOT: "Quit jumping on the bed!"

   - You do not have time to tell your children everything they should *not* do; this is an impossibly long list

4. **Be specific and direct; describe the behavior you want in simple, concrete terms:**

   - "Please put those blocks in the toy box." NOT: "You need to pick up a little bit in here."

   - Do not make the child guess what is important to you. Tell them.

5. **With younger children, give only one instruction at a time at first, adding more steps as the child demonstrates the ability to handle more:**

   - "Please put those blocks in the toy box" (wait until the toys are in the box); "Thank you! Now please put your shoes in the closet" (wait until the shoes are in the closet); "Great job! Now put your books back on the bookshelf." NOT: "Please put those blocks in the toy box, then put your shoes in the closet and the books back on the bookshelf, then go upstairs and get your pajamas and brush your teeth."

   - Often, children will remember only the first or last item from a long list of instructions.

6. **Give the command only once; then wait five to ten seconds for the child to respond:**

- The first time you give a command is information, the second time is nagging.

- Give the instruction, then count silently to yourself. If you count out loud, you will teach the child to wait until you are almost done counting before responding.

- If the child follows your instruction, show your appreciation by thanking them enthusiastically, giving them a high five, and so on. Make it obvious that you appreciate when the child listens.

- If the child does not follow the instruction, enforce compliance using the procedures outlined in the Time-Out procedure described in chapter 8

- This is not the time for discussion or explanations of the rules; rely on action, not talking.

7. **Be careful about giving commands you are not prepared to enforce:**

   - If the child learns you will enforce commands only some of the time, he or she will continue to test you to see if this is one of those times.

Written Expectations

When children are younger, telling them what you want them to do at the time you want them to do it can work well. Most little kids don't think or plan too far ahead anyway, so focusing on what is in front of them at that moment makes sense.

As they get a little more independent, though, their activities get more involved and time consuming. A lot of dissatisfaction and conflict happens when parents continue a pattern of telling their kids they need to do something "right now" when the kid knows the task could be done any time.

Kids complain to me that their parents interrupt their activities to give them instructions about something that really could wait until later. Not surprisingly, children tend to resent this. They think they are being disrespected. The message they hear is that their activities are not important or meaningful and that the parent only cares about their own agenda. Of course, there are times when something needs to be done promptly, but if every time you give an instruction it ends with you saying, "Right now," you are overdoing it, and resentment is probably brewing.

As kids get older and more sophisticated, we can add steps and complexity to their rules and chores. We also can give them more control over how the chores fit into their schedules. Rather than telling them to do the chore right away, we let them know when it needs to be done, giving children an opportunity to learn how to manage their own time and organize daily activities for themselves.

A lot of parents would say that if they don't tell the child what to do, it won't get done. This may be true, but the way to respond to this is not to tell the child what to do more often. When you do this, you are taking responsibility for the behavior instead of allowing them to be responsible. If the job doesn't get done, deliver a consequence, not a lecture.

When you write out a list of expectations and consequences, you are creating a simple contract. The basic terms of the contract are that if the child does what is expected, you will let them have their regular privileges and maybe something extra, like allowance. If they break a rule or do not get a chore done correctly or by the required time, they will lose their privileges and have to earn them back. In other words, their life goes on hold until the problem is fixed.

Basic written expectations might look something like the following example. Don't be too concerned about the specifics of the "Consequences" part at this point. You will see a reference to something called "Job Cards," a discipline tool that will be covered in more detail in the next section. The most important thing to recognize for now is that the "Rules" and "Chores" parts describe *child* responsibilities and the "Consequences" part details the *parent* responsibilities. If you want them to be reliable holding up their end of the deal, you must be just as reliable in holding up your end.

Expectations for Kaitlyn

Rules

- Follow instructions the first time.
- Use appropriate language (no yelling, arguing, name calling).
- Food and drink in the kitchen only.
- Two hours or less "screen time" daily (TV, computer and video games combined).
- Bedtime: 9:00 p.m. (in bed, lights out).

Chores

Daily:
- Make bed before eating breakfast.

- Load dishwasher right after dinner.

- Put dirty clothes in hamper by 6:00 p.m.

Weekly:
- Clean bedroom by noon Saturday.

- All clothes and personal items off the floor and put away appropriately

- Bed made

- Dust tops of dresser and chest

- Vacuum

- Collect trash and take to curb by 8:00 p.m. Wednesday.

Consequences

- Following all rules and completing all chores on time will earn all daily privileges and $3.00 per day payable by 5:00 p.m. Saturday.

- Breaking a rule or failing to complete a chore appropriately or on time will earn a loss of allowance, loss of all privileges for four hours and a Job Card.

- Privileges will be earned back when all three of the following are complete:

  1. The problem that earned the grounding is corrected (if possible)

2. At least four consecutive hours are spent without privileges

3. The Job Card is completed in an acceptable way

For some kids, turning the chore list into a chart or checklist helps them keep track of where they are in the process. Notice that each of the chores has an assigned time for completion. If the expectation is that the child's room should be clean by noon Saturday, they should have every opportunity to get it done without interference or reminders from you right up to noon. But if twelve o'clock rolls around and the room is not cleaned appropriately, the next thing that happens is a consequence, not a reminder. This puts the child in the position of having to learn how to organize and manage his or her own schedule and activities and eliminates arguments about your interrupting their activities to do chores "right this minute."

STEP 5: OZ OR KANSAS?

People sometimes seem to get the impression that the word *consequence* means the same thing as punishment or that only negative responses can be consequences. In fact, a consequence is just something that happens as a result of something else happening first, good or bad.

So punishment is one kind of consequence for behavior, and a reward is another kind of consequence. The point is that the consequence happens *because* the behavior happened first. It is a *result* of the child's behavior.

The essence of contrast is making "good" consequences happen in our children's lives when they choose to do what we want them to do and "bad" consequences when they do not. The greater the difference between the goodness of the "good things" and the badness of the "bad things," the easier their choice will be. If your children can't see that their life will change in some meaningful way as a result of how they choose to behave, they are not likely to be too concerned about making the right choice. Your job as a parent is to create consequences and follow through as promised, time after time. Their job is to make the choice.

> If your children can't see that their life will change in some meaningful way as a result of how they choose to behave, they are not likely to be too concerned about making the right choice.

Here is another way to think about it. Remember the movie *The Wizard of Oz*? When your children are behaving in ways you like, their lives should be like Oz—lots of color and pleasant sounds, interesting people and plenty of enjoyable sights and activities. But when they misbehave, it's Kansas: Dull. Flat. Black and white. Boring. Kansas. However, the doorway is always in front of them and it is in their power to get back to Oz. All they need to do is accept the discipline and get back on track. We only make the door available. It is up to them whether or not to open it.

So we could sum up the process of using consequences to create contrast (and most of this book for that matter) like this:

---

1. **If you see a behavior you like, pay attention to it and reward or reinforce it.**

2. **If you see a behavior you don't like, ignore or punish it.**

3. **Repeat.**

Levels of Consequences

Natural Consequences: Consequences happen at three different levels and children should experience all three. The first, natural consequences, are those that happen without any involvement by the parent. When your daughter rides her bike too fast, falls down and scrapes a knee, this is a natural consequence. When your child fails to observe classroom rules and has to stay after school, this is a natural consequence. The parent does not have to do anything (other than stay out of the way) for these consequences to occur.

Some of my older clients encounter more serious natural consequences like problems with the legal system. When you can see a natural consequence coming and also see that it will be painful, but not harmful or damaging, *let it happen.* Your child will learn much more from the experience than they would if you protected them from the consequence and just talked about it later.

Natural consequences are the most useful because they are most like what we experience as adults. Keep in mind that, like all other consequences, natural consequences can also operate in a positive direction. Getting good grades is a natural consequence of academic effort. Moving your belt in a notch is a natural consequence of eating more salads and fewer donuts. Of course, natural consequences are not always available, may not occur soon enough to be useful (like health problems from smoking, or belt problems from donuts) or may be too serious for you to allow them to happen.

Logical Consequences: The next level of possible consequences is usually referred to as logical consequences. These are consequences chosen by a parent or other adult, but having some logical relationship to the behavior. Unlike natural consequences, logical consequences do require some level of involvement by the parent. Suppose a child leaves his toy out on the floor after it is supposed to be put away. The parent picks up the toy and puts it out of reach somewhere. When the child asks about it later, the parent says something like, "You did not pick up your toy, so you will not be able to play with it for the rest of the day." Another example might be having to scrub all the walls in a room after drawing on one of them with crayons. The consequence is related in a logical, understandable way. Extending a curfew because your child has observed the current curfew consistently is a more positive example.

When you are able to come up with a logical consequence for a particular behavior and it would not be harmful or damaging, use it. Often though, it is not possible to deliver an appropriate logical consequence in a timely way. Sometimes, there is just no way to make the punishment fit the crime.

Intentional Consequences: The final level of consequences is intentional consequences. These are the consequences that are planned in advance for use in situations where natural or logical consequences are not available or will not occur soon enough to be useful. Examples of intentional consequences that will be described in the next section include Time-Out and Job Card Grounding and, on the positive side, allowance. Two important features of intentional consequences are (1) parents decide in advance what the consequences will look like and how strong they will be, and (2) they can be used for just about any situation.

Consequence History

If children are used to having lots of privileges and lots of attention from parents, they are likely to notice more quickly and experience more discomfort when all those things are removed. Big contrast = faster learning. Many of the families I work with are affectionate and attentive and their kids have gotten used to having lots of toys and other items to play with and enjoy. As often as not, the main struggle for parents in these families is to be more assertive and consistent in withholding these privileges when children have not met expectations.

In other families, children receive little notice or recognition when they are doing well. The first thing I work on with these families is getting parents to acknowledge and encourage their children's good behavior. Sometimes there does not seem to be too much good behavior to recognize. But the child is not likely to develop more good behavior if the few appropriate things they already do never get noticed or rewarded. And, if they rarely have privileges and are ignored most of the time anyway, they don't have much to lose by misbehaving. You can't lose what you don't have.

The response might be as simple as increasing the amount of praise or touch. Sometimes I ask parents to set aside a specific amount of time each day to devote to one-on-one, structured interactions with their child. At other times, we might set up a more formal system of small toys or trinkets, extra curfew time or an allowance. Often we begin by responding more positively to behaviors that seem only okay or just acceptable.

The author of a book on a very successful employee motivation program based on rewards puts it this way:

> Saying "Thank you" and "You're welcome" is bedrock communication. In my experience, if someone says "Thank you" often enough, it's pretty hard not to say "You're welcome." … If the objective were to say thank you as often as possible, it seemed we should design a way of saying "Thank you" to employees who did, day-in, day-out, what they were supposed to do: "Thank you for coming to work." "Thank you for not being late." (D.C. Boyle, *Secrets of a Successful Employee Recognition System: The 100 Point Solution.*

At home, this might be translated as, "Thank you for playing quietly" or "Thank you for coming when I called." At school, it might sound more like, "Thank you for having your materials ready" or "Thank you for completing your work on time." If reliable, productive, routine behavior is desired, then reliable, productive, routine behavior should be rewarded, not ignored.

Responding more reliably to a child's acceptable behavior serves two main purposes. First, and most important, more positive responses to appropriate behavior improve the overall relationship and increase the child's interest in interacting with the parent. The child sees the parent as being the "giver of good things." Second, when the overall value of the child's environment increases, there is greater contrast and improved learning when all of the attention and privileges are removed.

Rewards and Privileges

What makes a good reward? I have no idea. Okay, that is not completely true, but the reality is that there is no "one size fits all" list of things that all children will find rewarding or reinforcing.

I like chocolate. Most kids I know also like chocolate, but I have met some kids who don't like chocolate. I don't have much use for video games, but video games are even better than chocolate to a lot of kids I know. Most young kids like attention, but I have worked with some children with autism who would do just about anything to avoid contact with other people. The point is that what makes a good reward is that it is rewarding. That's it. It's not what I think or what you think should be rewarding that matters. Whatever your child finds interesting, enjoyable or exciting is a potential reward. These are the items and activities your child is most likely to be willing to work for and not want to lose.

> If reliable, productive, routine behavior is desired, then reliable, productive, routine behavior should be rewarded, not ignored.

One good way to figure out what might be reinforcing to your child is to watch their choices. When they are allowed to do what they want, what do they choose to do? When they are allowed to choose what they eat, what do they choose? When they have a chance to choose among friends, which friend is invited over first? Do they care about money, buying things or renting games or movies? Chances are good that the answer to these questions will tell you what they value and what activities and items can be used to motivate them.

Removing Privileges

When I think about planned or intentional consequences for unacceptable behavior, I usually think in terms of taking away *all* privileges (or at least all the privileges I am sure I can control), but for only a short time. For many kids, if I were to take away one or two privileges, there would still be a lot of privileges left. Not much contrast would be created, and I would not have done my job of presenting a clear choice. Most of the time it is much better to remove *all* privileges for a short time than some privileges for a long time.

So what exactly is a privilege? In my view, children are entitled to have their needs met, but should have to earn the rest. They are entitled to food, shelter, safety and love (though not necessarily attention). Everything else is a privilege and should be subject to being removed temporarily if expectations are not being met.

Timing of Consequences

In general, it is best to respond to behavior (appropriate or not) as quickly as possible, especially with younger children.

> They are entitled to food, shelter, safety and love (though not necessarily attention). Everything else is a privilege and should be subject to being removed temporarily if expectations are not being met.

Toddlers and preschoolers are very much "here and now" people, and they tend to think that whatever happens a few *seconds* after a behavior is the result of the behavior. If they cry and you pick them up, they will believe that crying gets them picked up. If complaining about what you made for lunch results in your taking it away and making something else, they are likely to complain more because complaining results in a lunch they like better. If you give them a "high five" right after they pick up their toys, they will think picking up toys gets them attention and praise.

Until the age of seven or so, most children have not developed the ability to think in an abstract way. If you delay consequences for hours or days, they are likely to lose the connection between the behavior and the outcome. As children mature, they are better able to understand that you are giving a consequence for a behavior that happened earlier.

Sometimes, we might use calendars, charts or some other "scorekeeping" system to keep track of behavior over time and then deliver the consequences periodically. In general, even with adolescents, it is best to focus on dealing with "today's behavior today" and move on to tomorrow, but setting up longer term goals and consequences can add another level of motivation and help children learn to delay gratification. Charts or tokens can help younger children bridge the time gap until they get the actual reward. So a child might earn a sticker or a mark on the calendar each day, but be allowed to "cash in" for a bigger item only once a week.

Delivering Consequences

If you want to create the greatest possible contrast, you must pay attention not only to what consequences you deliver and when, but also *how* you deliver them. When you respond to behaviors you like, do it with enthusiasm—you should be doing what I sometimes call the "good behavior happy dance." I tell parents to respond to behaviors they like in a way they would be embarrassed to do in front of me. Make it interesting as well as rewarding for your child to behave well, and you increase the chances for appropriate behavior. Again, this is especially true for younger children, but a little enthusiasm can go a long way even with adolescents.

When you respond to behaviors you do not like, follow the gravity model. Absolutely reliable. No warnings, explanations or discussion. No expressed anger or yelling. Be a force of nature. This emotionally neutral approach is important not only to help improve contrast with your more demonstrative reaction to appropriate behavior, but also to help protect you from being drawn into emotionally charged exchanges, which distract you from the real issues.

If your child learns that you get "wound up" when he or she misbehaves, this will become a tool for them to use to manage *your* behavior. Some kids are what I call "emotional vampires"— the more emotional you become, the more they feed off it and increase the intensity of their own emotional response. The more you turn it up, the more they turn it up. Your disciplinary efforts will go much better if you take all of that emotion and load it into responding when your child is doing well, instead of when they are misbehaving.

There are two ways to respond to behaviors you do not like; both should involve this emotionally neutral approach, and both create a change (contrast) from the child's regular life. If your child does something that annoys you, but you can tolerate, it may be best just to ignore it. Basically, the idea is simply to remove any payoff in the form of attention or emotion. Stop paying someone and they eventually stop coming to work. If you can't tolerate a behavior or if it was on your list of "non-negotiable" expectations, you should punish it by removing privileges using one of the tools described in the next section or something similar.

The second important issue in delivering consequences is that you present an alternative. It is not enough to tell the child what was done wrong; they also should be told what they could do instead. If they earn a consequence for breaking a rule, the next step may be as simple as reminding them of the rule and letting them know how they can earn their privileges back. If they lost privileges because they failed to complete a task, they should be given an opportunity to complete the task. Remember, punishment tells a child what not to do, but does not tell them what to do instead. All of these components are contained in the next few paragraphs discussing the idea of Deliberate Discipline.

STEP 6: PRACTICE DELIBERATE DISCIPLINE

Parents are much more likely to follow through with disciplinary and motivational actions if they decide two important details ahead of time: (1) what behaviors they are going to respond to and (2) how they are going to respond. In other words, they have a plan. It probably is useful if the child has this information ahead of time as well, but it is not essential.

Remember, gravity *never* gives warnings, yet every normally developing child figures out how it works. The more important issues are your commitment to the process and how closely you follow the procedures you have decided on from one teaching opportunity to the next. The more consistent you are, the more quickly your children will get the idea and the more sense the world will make to them.

What to Discipline

Broken Rules: In my view, any behavior you think of as unacceptable *can* be subject to discipline, but those behaviors you have identified in advance as unacceptable *must* be disciplined. This, in part, is why I suggest you keep your list of expectations short and avoid including behaviors you cannot enforce. If you have too many items on your list, you will probably forget some or be less consistent or rigorous about enforcing them. Either way, you end up looking less capable and more ineffective to the child. If they find that you do not respond sometimes, they are more likely to test the next time. Better to have a few requirements you enforce consistently than many you enforce once in a while.

You may have heard someone say you should "pick your battles." The idea seems to be that you should let most minor misbehavior go and focus only on more serious issues. This is a mistake. Little things matter. A history lesson might be useful here. In 1994, the Mayor of New York City hired a new police commissioner, a man who had dramatically reduced crime on the city subway system. How?

Instead of focusing on big things such as muggings and assaults, he emphasized cleaning up graffiti and arresting those who did not pay their $1.25 subway fare (about 170,000 a day at one point). The result? The new culture of no tolerance for *any* rule-breaking resulted in a dramatic decrease in *all* kinds of crime, including assaults and robberies. Clamping down on littering, public urination and minor property damage led to similar huge decreases in overall crime rates in the city. Little things matter.

Work to establish an understanding in your home that following instructions, even little ones, is expected and will be enforced, but also appreciated. Make sure that, if you tell your child to take his or her dishes to the sink or pick up their socks, this gets done. For one thing, it is a lot easier to get your child to do something that is not that difficult and this helps establish a habit of compliance. Salesmen call this the "foot in the door" technique. You are more likely to get someone to go along with a big request if they have already gone along with a smaller one. On the other hand, just letting it go or doing it yourself (because it's just easier) sets you up for more serious violations later.

When it comes to rules, my suggestion is that two kinds of infractions must be disciplined reliably and without hesitation: (1) not following a direct instruction (verbal or written), and (2) any kind of aggressive behavior (including aggressive language or actions against property, pets or people). Things you definitely should *not* discipline are unintentional or accidental behavior or situations where the child really has no control over events or which are truly "can't do" behaviors.

Late or Incomplete Chores: Chores are either done appropriately and on time or they are not. If you have outlined how and when a chore is to be completed, you have done your part and the rest is up to the child. If the time comes for the chore to be done and it is not, a consequence should follow, even if it is only a minute late, even if the child says he or she will do it right away.

If the child misses a step or does not complete the chore fully, either because he or she is just learning the procedure or because you did not explain it well enough, you might allow an exception. In this case, tell them that they did a good job overall, but missed a step. Then tell them that, because they are just learning (or because you did not give them enough information), you will not give them a consequence this time. Then tell them what they should change or improve the next time to avoid the consequence.

A common argument by adolescents and children is that it is incredibly unfair to be punished for being "just a few minutes late" getting home or for not quite getting a chore done. This is an area where parents seem to give in with some regularity. It might help to consider some of the kind of "grown-up world" examples you are trying to prepare your children for.

Example 1: You can get to the airport as early as you want, but if you get there after they close the airplane door, it's too late.

The last one on still gets to go, but whether you miss the flight by a minute or an hour, the outcome is the same, you still stay on the ground.

Example 2: You can pay your taxes any time before midnight on April 15, but April 16 is too late, and there will be a financial consequence for your tardiness. Apologies and promises to do better might be appreciated, but you will still get the bill.

If one of the assigned chores is to take out the trash by 6:00 p.m., your child should be allowed every second up to 6:00 to get it done, but 6:01 is too late, and a consequence should be given. If curfew is midnight, 12:01 a.m. is too late, and a consequence should be given. If you start to allow a little "wiggle room" in these deadlines, you will almost certainly end up with more disagreements and resistance when you do decide to follow through.

It is important that you be as good as your word. If you "promise" a consequence, good or bad, be sure you deliver it. If you expect your child to be reliable, you must model reliability in your interactions with the child.

Deliberate Discipline Steps

A deliberate approach to discipline requires a consistent method for teaching or training interactions. Each teaching interaction, from preschool through high school, should include the following components:

Step 1.   Identify the problem

Step 2.   Deliver a consequence

Step 3.   Establish a goal for future behavior

Step 4.   Add an "earn back" provision

Identify the Problem: If you have communicated your expectations clearly, this step should not take long. If you gave an instruction that was not followed, the only thing you need to say is, "You're not listening." If a household rule was broken or a chore not completed on time or in the way required, you only have to point to the rule on the list or remind the child of what it says. If you cannot clearly identify what the problem is using around seven words or fewer, you probably have not refined your expectations well enough.

Be brief and focus on the current behavior, not on what the child has done before. If you find yourself using words like *always* and *never* to describe behavior, you will need to sharpen your focus. Remember, the first time you describe the problem behavior provides the necessary information; the second time is nagging.

Of course, if either you or your child is unclear about what is expected, this step is more likely to turn into an argument. The parent tells the child they have broken a rule. The child says something like, "You never said that," or some other, more creative response. The parent argues back or begins to doubt whether they really did say what they thought, and so on. Eventually there is a full-blown meltdown, or the parent gives in after making some comment about what will happen next time if this keeps up.

This step and the next are the most likely places for your child to try to draw you into a discussion or to increase the emotional volume to distract you from the issue at hand. Do your best to maintain a calm, matter-of-fact approach. Focus on the process and try not to be drawn into discussions about "content" or emotionally charged exchanges.

Deliver a Consequence: If you have worked out a plan for how you will respond to your child's behavior, this should be a simple (but not necessarily easy) step. If the behavior already has resulted in a natural consequence for the child, you may want to just point it out to them, tell them how they might go about fixing it, then leave it alone. Usually, it is best to resist the temptation to "pile on." If you are able to come up with a logical and proportional consequence, let them know what the consequence is and the rationale for it. For example, "You left your bike outside last night, so I am locking it up in the garage today."

Most of the time, natural and logical consequences are hard to come by, and you will be using an intentional or planned consequence of some kind, usually Time-Out or Job Card Grounding or something similar (see the next section). If you use the same approach consistently, your kids will become accustomed to the procedure, and you should not have much to explain about the "cost" of their inappropriate actions or what they will need to do to earn their privileges back. They will already know because it will be the same as the time before and the time before that.

Establish a Goal for Future Behavior: Once you have identified the problem behavior and the consequence, let the child know what you expect them to do instead in the future. Most of the time, this will involve simply restating a rule you have already listed (or asking the child to restate it) or clarifying how a chore needs to be done differently the next time. If possible, you might even practice the goal behavior. For example, show the child how the chore needs to be done differently next time and have them practice the appropriate steps.

Sometimes practice can also be a consequence. When the child does something that breaks the rules and is more physical in nature (like slamming doors, running down the hall or stomping up the stairs), a technique called *positive practice* can be useful. This involves having your child do the appropriate action correctly (like closing the door softly, walking slowly down the hall or going quietly up the steps) ten times. I'm not sure why, but ten seems to be the magic number for some reason. It is usually best to arrange this practice at a time when your child has something else they are eager to get to. They are more likely to cooperate if they know their friend is waiting to play, their favorite TV show is on or their girlfriend called and is expecting a call back.

Add an "Earn Back" Requirement: Remember, the purpose of punishment is to reduce or eliminate behavior, not to create new behaviors. It helps your child learn what not to do, but not what to do instead. Obviously, it is important that your kids learn that it will cost them something if they do not follow your rules or instructions, but it is even more important that they experience earning something when they do listen. This is the purpose of requiring them to do something to earn back their privileges.

If the child did not follow a direction or did not get a chore done, they would be expected to do whatever they were told before or finish the chore and maybe a little more to get off punishment. If the problem is not fixable, they would be expected to do some other positive, useful, helpful act to "earn back" their privileges.

Every planned disciplinary interaction, from a toddler's first Time-Out to an adolescent's last grounding, should end the same way, with a parent saying, "Nice job. You can have your privileges back." In other words, the last step is for you to recognize and reinforce appropriate behavior. Without this step, you do not have a complete training interaction.

This step also makes children active participants in the disciplinary process. They must *do something* in order to get their life back, not just wait. Discipline does not just happen to them; they are involved. It also introduces an element of control that makes sense to most kids. If they don't feel like earning their their privileges back right away, they don't have to. Skilled parents are willing to let their children go without privileges for as long as they might choose knowing that, eventually, they will probably get tired of having no life and make a decision to accomplish whatever is needed to earn their stuff back.

At this point, the parent responds as if the child has just done them the greatest favor one human being has ever done for another, congratulates them on their good sense and restores their privileges. This positive attention along with getting privileges back creates a sharp and immediate contrast with the child's previous situation.

You may have noticed that the first letters in each step spell out the word *IDEA: Identify, Deliver, Establish and Add.* This might be an easy way to remember the steps.

SIX

What to Do When You Like What They Do

B y the time families get to my office, a lot of parents have developed what I call the "no" bias. Their initial response to child requests is almost always "no," sometimes even before the child has finished asking the question. Then, at least some of the time, the child whines long enough or badgers the parent into changing their mind and giving them what they want.

Saying "yes" under these circumstances rarely feels good to the parent. Often, these parents are upset with themselves for giving in and become even more determined to say "no" to more requests more quickly, and the cycle repeats and intensifies.

Mostly what children in this situation learn is to ignore the first "no" and to be more forceful and persistent in bullying the parent. Both parent and child gear up for a negative interaction before they even start to talk.

I encourage parents to try to develop a "yes" bias or, more accurately a "yes, if" bias. Instead of an automatic negative reaction, I encourage them to make this their default response to child requests: "Yes you can do what you want if you have done what you were supposed to." Or, in other words, "Yes you can have some ice cream if you have eaten your broccoli."

This puts the responsibility squarely back on the child. What the parent is communicating is that they are more than willing to let the child do things they want to do (as long as it is within the rules). It is really up to the child to determine whether or not they actually get the chance because they get to decide either to do what they are supposed to or not.

The most important point here is that we *want* our children to have privileges, lots of them. If they have privileges, they have something to lose and are easier to motivate. If they have privileges, they are probably going to be easier to get along with. We just don't want them to have privileges they have not earned. We do want to respond reliably to their appropriate behaviors in ways that let them know we approve of and appreciate what they did. Like most other methods we have talked about, you are more likely to do this if you have equipped yourself with tools in advance.

BEHAVIORAL TOOLS

Owning a hammer does not make you a carpenter. Not everyone who has a pen in their drawer can be a novelist. In other words, tools are great, but they work best if you have some understanding of how to use them. To this point, we have focused more on general principles of learning and behavior. Now that we have the background, we can begin to get more specific.

This chapter and the next include descriptions of several common tools for discipline and motivation. These are the intentional consequences you will use when natural or logical consequences are not readily available or appropriate. Each of the methods recommended is used commonly in pediatric behavioral psychology and has been used for years in my own practice. Each is built on the concepts and principles presented in the previous chapters.

These time-tested, tried-and-true techniques are good enough that, even if you did not know anything about behavior, you probably would still get some improvement just by following the directions. The problem would come when things did not go exactly as planned (which happens to everyone) and you had to make some adjustments. Better to know how and why the tools are designed the way they are.

Unfortunately, no tool or method can be used with every child in every situation, but the following techniques have been demonstrated to be effective for the majority of children. Even if you have to tweak the specific steps a little to fit your situation, as long as you follow the fundamental principles you have learned, you should be good.

If you have a difficult or willful child, plan to spend extra time working to increase the number and quality of your positive responses to the child before you implement more assertive discipline. Increase the value and interest of their daily lives, and they will have more to lose by misbehaving and more to earn back by correcting their behavior. Pay attention to how you respond and what you say to your child throughout the day. A good rule of thumb is to make *at least* twice as many positive or praise statements and actions as negative or corrective responses.

It can be hard to find things to reinforce with kids who have a high level of problem behavior. It is easy to develop a habit of watching for bad behavior and not noticing good or just acceptable behavior. When this happens, the child gets used to having mostly negative interactions with adults and begins to avoid them or tune them out. If there is a history of this kind of situation, you will have to make a conscious effort to notice acceptable behaviors more often. In other words, you will have to begin by trying to change your own habits. When there is a long-standing pattern of difficult interactions between a parent and a child, positive change almost always has to start with the adult.

The fact that parents may have to make changes in how they interact with a child does not necessarily mean they have been doing something "wrong." Think of it this way. You might be a wonderful cook who prepares delicious and nutritious meals every day. But if you have a child who is diabetic, you probably will have to change the way you cook. It does not mean you were doing something wrong before, it just means that there was a bad "fit" between what you were doing and the child's needs.

> When there is a long-standing pattern of difficult interactions between a parent and a child, positive change almost always has to start with the adult.

In my office I often see parents who have responded to behavior in reasonable and appropriate ways and the child is still misbehaving. If they want a different result, they have to change the way they cook. Here are some recipes you may want to try.

TIME-IN

Time-In is the name we give to the overall collection of privileges children may enjoy when they are behaving acceptably. If your child is not exposed to regular and rich Time-In experiences, Time-Out will not work because there will be no meaningful contrast. Regular (but not unregulated) access to toys and other activities is a big part of Time-In.

> The better the Time-In, the more powerful the Time-Out.

In general, materials that require some creativity or input by the child or some physical activity are better than toys or electronics that can be played with in only one way. Television and some other electronic items encourage the child to be a passive recipient rather than an active participant in the environment.

For young children, positive attention from a caregiver is the most valuable part of the Time-In, and physical touch is one of the more important aspects of positive attention. Keeping a high level of positive attention and positive interactions with your child will not only help to improve your relationship and your child's sense of security, but also set the stage for more productive discipline. The better the Time-In, the more powerful the Time-Out.

To be most effective in helping your child learn to behave acceptably, positive attention should be given whenever you notice the child doing anything that is *acceptable* to you. There is no need to be stingy with praise, positive comments and touch. They are free, portable and you never run out of them. Parent behaviors that increase the overall level of positive attention and the "richness" of the Time-In environment include proximity, brief touch and praise:

Proximity: At least some of the time during your daily activities, place your child close to you so it is easy to reach him or her. Organize and promote activities, routines, and a schedule that will keep the child near you so little or no extra effort is required on your part to maintain contact. Keep the child close in the car, at the market, during meals, and so on. As you begin to encourage more independent play, check on the child periodically rather than waiting for him or her to come to you.

> There is no need to be stingy with praise, positive comments and touch. They are free, portable and you never run out of them.

Brief Touch: Frequent and brief touch (one or two seconds) will do more to demonstrate your approval than any amount of talking. Train yourself to touch or pat your child gently on the shoulder, head or back twenty-five to fifty times a day, but *only* at times when their behavior is *acceptable*. Your touch is a way to let children know you are aware of their activities and that you approve of what they are doing, but without interrupting them. Doing this fifty times requires less than two minutes of your time! You can include a positive comment like, "I like the way you are playing quietly," but this is not essential. Your touch alone communicates a great deal.

Labeled Praise: Describe briefly and specifically what you like about the child's behavior. This helps the child to learn what actions will result in more positive attention. For example: "I like the way you cleaned up the bathroom after your shower. Thanks!" is better than a simple statement such as, "Thanks," but some praise is better than none at all.

Third-party Praise: Look for opportunities to let your child "overhear" your positive comments to someone else about his or her good behavior or accomplishments. Suggest they show their math paper or artwork to their other parent or grandparents. "Publicize" their efforts by putting the papers up on the refrigerator, on a computer desktop or on the family website.

ALLOWANCE

There are many different ways to handle the process of helping your child learn about earning and managing money. Some parents provide a certain amount of money weekly or monthly whether a child is doing well or not and require them to pay their own expenses. Some provide a base amount of allowance and offer opportunities to earn more by doing extra chores. Some parents "fine" their children for misbehavior by taking some of their allowance back. Some parents believe it is important to require their child to save a portion of their allowance or to make donations to church or charity. Others are more concerned about controlling purchases. There is no one "right" way to approach this issue.

My usual recommended approach is to allow the child an opportunity to earn a daily allowance just by taking care of regular responsibilities when and how they are supposed to. I recommend parents award or withhold allowance daily depending on whether rules were followed and chores were completed correctly and on time.

In other words, if the child earns allowance for taking care of routine responsibilities. This fits into the general approach of dealing with behavior on a day-by-day basis. I usually recommend parents take care of the child's regular expenses such as school lunches, athletic fees and so on, but require them to use their own money for recreational activities or extra purchases. I discourage "lending" children money except in unusual circumstances. In general, I might start an allowance at about the time I move to more of a privilege-based disciplinary system, usually around age eight or so.

Most adults earn their pay by showing up for work and doing what they are supposed to do. If they do something special or work overtime, they expect a bonus or a raise. It is certainly reasonable to allow your child to earn extra money by doing extra chores, but in my view, reinforcing regular effort is the more important goal.

Here are some guidelines you may want to consider in setting up an allowance:

- Decide on an amount of money you are willing to make available to your child each week. If helping them learn to save or make donations is important to you, be sure to consider this and be sure to allow enough that they can still have a little cash after they save or give some. It may be useful for you to keep track of how much money you actually give them for a week or two before deciding on this amount. You may be surprised at how much money you hand out just because you were asked.

- Divide the weekly allowance by seven (six if you want to give them a chore-free Sunday) and let the child know that this amount can be earned every day just by following rules and completing chores appropriately. Identify a time each week when allowance will be paid and make sure you follow through with timely payment. If you expect them to save or to make a donation to church or charity, be sure you keep a written record or chart of savings or donations to reinforce how the amount grows over time. Using a clear glass or plastic bank for savings helps the child visualize how their money is accumulating.

- On days the child meets expectations, mark your calendar or a chart with your initials indicating allowance has been earned for that day. If expectations were not met, tell them they will have a chance to start over tomorrow.

  - For younger children, it is sometimes more effective to give a token of some kind (a poker chip, a marble) that can be redeemed later. If you are skilled with a computer, you can create "family money" for each child and hand it out each night. Be sure to use methods that will not tempt children to either steal from each other or try to "counterfeit." Different colored poker chips for each child or requiring your signature on family money usually meet this goal. The additional advantage of this kind of system is that you might allow the child to use their tokens or family money to buy privileges.

 – It will seem like a bigger deal to younger children if you pay up with four quarters or ten dimes rather than a dollar bill. This also makes it easier to divide the portion that goes to savings or a donation.

 – Consider "settling up" on a Saturday or Sunday night when the child has less chance to go out and spend the money right away.

• When the child asks to do some activity or buy something, make your answer, *"Yes if* you have done what you are responsible for that day and you have the money." If either or both of those conditions have not been met, then the child would not be allowed to participate.

• Review the amount of the allowance from time to time. As children move into their pre-teen years, you may want to increase the amount, but also increase the number of things they must pay for out of their own funds. A big part of making this determination will be how responsibly they have handled their money to that point.

GRAB BAG OR TREASURE BOX

Just like adults, kids like to get new things and extra privileges. Setting up a system that allows them to "earn" extra items and activities helps them learn to associate positive outcomes with their effort. In other words, *First the Broccoli, Then the Ice Cream.* If you set up a Grab Bag or Treasure Box with some small treats or trinkets, you can use this either to help reward a new behavior that is being learned (for example, earning a Grab Bag treat for sleeping all night in their own bed) or for rewarding "good days" (following rules and completing chores).

Creating a list of items and assigning a "price" to each one can help the child learn to delay gratification or save toward a bigger goal. Here's how that might be done:

Preparation

1. **Develop a list of items the child will be interested in earning. Write down any small, easily delivered rewards you can think of. Ask your child to help you think of rewards.**

2. **Create twenty-five to fifty slips of paper, each about the same size (half of an index card works well). On each paper, write down one of the rewards from the list. Consider the following categories:**

   Food and drink
   - These will be most interesting if they are items your children do not get regularly or if this is the only way they can be earned.

   - Examples: Candy, raisins, nuts, soda pop, ice cream, drink boxes

   Social
   - These are often the best type of incentive as they provide for planned, one-on-one attention from a parent or caregiver

   - Write down amounts of time ranging from five to thirty minutes and identify the person with whom the time can be spent (for example, ten minutes of mom's time, fifteen minutes of dad's time)

- You may also want to identify an activity that will be of interest to both the child and the parent (such as fifteen minutes playing basketball with dad)

Privileges
- Examples: Extra "screen" time (TV, computer, video games), stay up 15 minutes late, chore free day

Things to Buy
- Examples: Hot Wheels car, hair care items (barrettes, "scrunchies"), stickers, fancy pencils

- If the child is interested in money, this can be a constructive way to provide it. Use different amounts of money (nickel, dime, quarter) and make several cards with each amount. Include one grand prize card with a large amount of money (anywhere from $1 to $5). Let your child know this card is in the bag and that if it is drawn, he or she will get that much money.

Procedure

1. **Place the papers in a jar, bag or bowl.**

2. **When your child meets a goal for behavior, allow him or her to "pull from the Grab Bag."**

3. **The child closes his or her eyes and pulls out a slip of paper at random.**

4. **After your child selects a reward, the card should be returned to the bag (if the grand prize is pulled, you might want to hold it out for a few days).**

5. **Consider having a "mystery bonus day" once a week, where the child will be allowed to draw twice if their behavior has been acceptable (the child should not know in advance which day will be the bonus day).**

6. **Be sure that pulls from the Grab Bag are accompanied by lots of praise and positive comments about the child's success at meeting his or her goals for behavior.** Do not negotiate for an exchange of items if the child does not get the desired item. Tell them they will have another chance the next day.

7. **For older children, it may be useful to have an "IOU" option: the child may either choose to take a smaller Grab Bag item right now or choose family money or another token that can be saved up and used to purchase big ticket items.** Some parents will buy an item their child asks for while shopping, set a "price" on the item and not allow the child to have it until they have enough tokens to redeem. I have known families who keep track of their children's earnings on a checkbook ledger, and, when the time comes to cash in at the treasure box, they check their balance to see if they have adequate funds.

Suggestions for Rewards/Reinforcers

Activities

Extra TV time

Choose video or TV program

Extra phone time

Extra video game time

Extra computer/Internet time

Stay up late

Sleep in

Special time or activity with a parent

Go to the park

Stay over with a friend

Have a friend over

Have a friend spend the night

Go to the mall

Time alone

Visit a relative

Trip to library

Sleep or eat in family room

Bike ride

Wear preferred clothes

Paint fingernails

Wear cologne or perfume

Access to art or craft supplies

Blow bubbles

Play in the lawn sprinkler

Bubble bath

Picnic on the lawn

Slumber party in parents' room

Bake cookies

Fishing

Swimming

Skating

Gym or YMCA time

Concert

Sporting event

Movie

Video or video game rental

Summer camp

Lessons (piano, guitar, karate)

Car/Driving

Drive with mom or dad

Use the car

Money toward insurance

Money toward car payment

Learner's permit

Driver's license

Food and Drink

Choose dinner menu

Order a pizza

Fast food dinner

Candy

Cookies

Dinner out

Ice cream

Soft drink (pop)

Things to Buy

CDs or DVD

MP3 player

Cell phone

Video game

Art supplies

Clothes or shoes

Dolls or accessories

Bike, scooter, etc.

Football, baseball, etc.

Get hair or nails done

Manicure

Hair accessories

At School

Hand out/collect papers

First in line

Sit by teacher

Extra recess

Bring a pet to school

Feed classroom pet

Help janitor

Cafeteria helper

Lunch with teacher

Get a drink pass

Play cards/game with principal

Play cards/game with a friend

Choose book for story time

Visit another classroom

At School (cont.)	Miscellaneous
Display picture or special achievement on bulletin board	Get out of grounding
	Skip a chore/chore-free day
Phone call home to report achievement	Get a pet
	Decorate room
Share a special toy or book from home with class	Get ears pierced
Special certificate	***Free or low-cost items**

SEVEN

What to Do When You Don't Like What They Do

I n the previous chapter, we looked at some ways to respond when your child is behaving in an acceptable or appropriate way. This chapter considers what to do when they are not.

As discussed numerous times throughout the book, the idea is to make it as obvious as possible to the child that you disapprove of their behavior, not by lecturing or nagging, but by making a big change in the quality of their life. The best way to accomplish this, of course, is to remove as many of their privileges as possible as soon as possible. The more items on the privileges list, the greater the contrast and the more powerful the message. If the child does not have many privileges, this probably won't have much effect.

If we want to create repetition by delivering the message often (and we do), the length of time we remove privileges should be relatively short. We want it to be clear to the child that privileges have been suspended or put on hold, not lost permanently, and that they can be earned back in a reasonable time if behavior improves. This provides more practice opportunities and the two key conditions for successful training (contrast and repetition) are met. Each of the methods includes the steps for Deliberate Discipline.

Many of the procedures suggested here are similar to what you might find elsewhere. You may even have tried something similar. Even if you are already using some version of the techniques described, please read the descriptions fully and carefully anyway. I have found that, over time, parents tend to "drift" from their original disciplinary methods, even if they were reasonably successful. They end up adding steps or leaving steps out and then wonder why the system does not seem to be working as well as it had. Sometimes the child does well for a long time and the parents think they are done with the heavy lifting of discipline and relax. They stop doing the very things that led to the improvement in the first place.

There is nothing magical about my particular approach to these disciplinary techniques, but if you follow the step-by-step instructions, you will meet the main requirements for effective discipline. This does not guarantee dramatically improved behavior, but it does dramatically increase your chances for success, especially if you stick with it over time.

If you have been struggling with discipline and motivation for some time, if you have a strong-willed child or if you are attempting to assert yourself as a parent for the first time, you should be aware of how your child may respond when you "turn up the heat."

Consider this analogy. Suppose you walk up to a candy machine or pop machine, put in your money, make your selection, press the button and nothing happens. No candy. No pop. What do you do next? If you are like most people, you press another button, then the coin return, then all the buttons. If there is still no result, you might pound on the buttons, or give the machine a little nudge or kick. You are used to putting something in (money) and getting something out in return (candy or pop), and you do not like it much when you do not get what you expect or think you deserve.

This is just the kind of button-pushing, machine-shaking reaction you might get from your children when you implement a more forceful approach to discipline. If they have been accustomed to having mostly free access to privileges or if they have been used to arguing or being obnoxious to get what they want, they are likely to respond just the way you would with the candy machine. When they put something in (arguing, obnoxious behavior), but don't get out what they expect (parents giving in), they may increase their argumentative or obnoxious behavior for a time. After all, it worked before. Don't be surprised if they "shake the machine a little" when you change things up.

The good news is that people do not keep shaking the machine forever. Eventually, they figure out that nothing is coming out and give up or try a more productive approach. If you hold the line and consistently refuse to reward argumentative or obnoxious behavior by giving in to it, there is a good chance your child will come around too. This will happen more quickly if you have given them some other, more appropriate way to get what they are after.

INTENTIONAL IGNORING

If your child does something you find annoying, but which you can tolerate, ignore it. If attention seeking is part of the reason the child is doing this behavior, you have taken away the payoff. This might be as simple pretending the behavior does not exist, turning away for a few seconds, leaving the room or occupying yourself with some other activity.

As soon as the child gets back to doing anything that is acceptable to you, *immediately* respond to them in a big and positive way. If the child is doing something potentially dangerous or damaging, interfere, but continue to ignore. Even if attention seeking is not the main reason for their behavior, you at least have not added to the problem by showing them they can get you to react.

SECONDHAND CONSEQUENCES

Over the years, there have been a few times when I found it really difficult to figure out an effective consequence for a child I was working with. It seemed as if no matter what the child was offered, they had no interest in working for it. Whatever privilege was removed, they seemed unaffected. Sometimes these children seem as content to play with a piece of lint or some other useless object they found lying around as anything else.

On several occasions, I found that the best thing I could do to motivate their behavior was not to remove privileges *from them* if they misbehaved, but to give extra privileges *to their siblings* if they misbehaved. These children did not seem to care that much one way or the other about what they had, but they could not stomach the idea of seeing their brother or sister benefit from their misbehavior.

TIME-OUT

Almost every parent of a young child who comes into my office tells me they are using Time-Out. Almost none of them actually are. They all do something they *call* Time-Out, but they have missed the point somehow.

Time-Out is not just sitting in a chair or in a bedroom for a few minutes. To be effective, Time-Out has to include all the elements we have talked about to this point. Time-Out means the child is moved from a fun, interesting and enjoyable situation to a dull, boring and uninteresting one. In other words, Time-Out is the loss of Time-In. It is Time-Out from positive reinforcement or reward. It is the extreme form of intentional ignoring. Properly implemented, Time-Out is among the most powerful intentional consequences you can use with children up to the age of seven or eight.

> Properly implemented, Time-Out is among the most powerful intentional consequences you can use with children up to the age of seven or eight.

Of all the privileges a child should lose during Time-Out, the most important is getting attention from and interacting with their parents. This seems to be a common problem area for adults who tend to want to talk to or lecture the child who is sitting in

Time-Out or after. Don't do it! In fact, as soon as you speak to the child, they are not really in Time-Out anymore because they are being given the thing they probably want most, your attention. Of course, if they are not getting much of your attention when they are doing well, they probably won't notice much if you don't attend to them while they are in Time-Out.

The procedure described here is similar to how most of my colleagues would suggest you do Time-Out and includes the most important training methods we have discussed. If you do your best to just follow the procedures as described, you have a good chance of being effective.

Preparation

1. **Make sure the child's regular environment (Time-In) is interesting and enjoyable to him or her. If it is not, Time-Out will be much less effective.**

2. **Make sure you are giving effective commands. It is not reasonable to hold a child accountable for expectations that are not made clear. If necessary, review the Guidelines for Effective Instructions.**

3. **Choose a place for Time-Out. Usually, an adult-sized chair placed in an out-of-the-way place, such as the hallway, kitchen or corner of a room works well.**

    -   Any place that will be dull and boring for the child (but not dark, scary or dangerous) is appropriate.

    -   The chair should be in a place where the child cannot see the TV, play with toys or other objects, or be involved in the activities of the home.

- If a chair is not available, sit the child on a step or the floor. It is usually best to reserve the child's room for a back-up (see below) rather than the main place for Time-Out.

- The goal is to have a disciplinary method that can be used at home, but also when you are away from home. Since you can't take your child's room with you when you go out, best not to train them to do discipline there.

4. **Decide which of your child's behaviors will result in Time-Out.**

- Make sure there is understanding and agreement among caregivers about this. This should include two classes of behavior: (1) doing something he or she was not supposed to do (throwing a toy, hitting a sibling), and (2) not doing something he or she was supposed to do (not following directions).

5. **Decide how long the child will remain in Time-Out.**

- Usually two or three minutes for preschoolers and five minutes for school-age children. Time-Outs longer than five minutes are not likely to produce significantly better results. As long as the child stays in the seat or in the general area of the seat, do not react. Their behavior while in Time-Out does not matter much as long as they are doing what they are supposed to (seated and quiet) when it is time to get up. Use the same length of time for every problem behavior.

Procedure

When the child does something you do not like, *immediately* do the following:

1. **If the child failed to follow an instruction within five to ten seconds, say "You are not listening, Time-Out."**

    • Say this only once in a calm, matter-of-fact way.

    • Once you have said the words "Time-Out," you will not speak to the child again until you are ready to release him or her.

    If the child did something he or she was not supposed to do like hitting or throwing a toy, say, "No (hitting, throwing toys), Time-Out."

    • Say this only once in a calm, matter-of-fact way.

    • Once you have said the words "Time-Out," you will not speak to the child again until you are ready to release him or her from Time-Out.

2. **Using the least amount of guidance possible, lead the child to the Time-Out chair or spot.**

    • Guidance may be anything from pointing to the chair, walking alongside the child, leading the child by the hand, or carrying the child.

3. **Require the child to stay in Time-Out for the amount of time you have decided. The child must be sitting quietly in the chair when the time is up in order to be released.**

    • During the time the child is in Time-Out, keep your interactions at an absolute minimum. Do not speak to the child or even look at the child during this time.

- In order to be released, the child must be seated and quiet when the time is over.

- If the child is talking, crying or otherwise not meeting the requirements for release when the time is up, ignore him or her, but be ready to release the child as soon as he or she quiets down.

If the child will not stay in the chair, try one of the following "back up" methods:

Put Backs: Using the least amount of guidance necessary, put the child back in the chair without saying a word or reacting in any other way that might be interesting to the child.

- You may have to repeat this numerous times the first few times you do it.

Room Back Up: Lead the child to a safe room (without talking) and close the door.

- Ignore any acting out while the child is in the room.

- When the child is quiet, open the door and say, "You are quiet now, you may come out."

- Return the child to the chair to finish Time-Out.

Walking Time-Out: Stop trying to directly enforce Time-Out, but begin at once to ignore the child in every way possible.

- Withhold every privilege you can control without being confrontational.

- When the child asks for a privilege or your help with something say, "You owe me a Time-Out."

- Continue to withhold attention and support until the child returns to the chair and completes the Time-Out.

4. **When the time is up and the child is quiet and in the chair, go to where the child is seated and say, "You are quiet, you may get up now."**

    - You, not the child, decide when he or she may get up.

    - If the child refuses to get up, say, "Then you stay there until I tell you to get up."

    - The next time you move to release the child, take him or her by the wrist and say, "You are quiet, you may get up now," and lift them to their feet.

5. **What happens next depends on what the child did to earn Time-Out.**

    If Time-Out was earned for not following an instruction, the child should immediately be given another chance to follow the same direction.

    - If the child does not comply, go back to Step 1 and repeat. If the child still has not complied by the third time you give the instruction, use physical guidance to help the child complete the task.

    - When the child does comply, give lots of positive attention (praise and touch), even if your help was needed to complete the task.

    If Time-Out was earned for doing something the child was not supposed to do (like throwing a toy, saying a bad word), give the child a simple task to do, such as handing something to you or picking up a toy. Make sure the task is something you can enforce with physical guidance if necessary.

    - If the child does not comply, go back to Step 1 and repeat.

- Follow the instructions for enforcing following instructions.

IMPORTANT! Your training interaction with the child is not over until the child has followed your instruction and you have had the chance to praise or otherwise reward the child!

6. **Once these five steps are complete, the child has a "clean slate" and should not be lectured or reminded about the behavior that earned the Time-Out.**

Time-Out Checklist

What to check if Time-Out does not seem to be working:

- Is the child's environment interesting and enjoyable when he or she is not in Time-Out?

- Are you giving effective instructions?

- Is the place you have chosen for Time-Out dull and boring (away from TV, toys, people and other distractions)?

- Are you calm when placing the child in Time-Out? If not, you may be waiting too long to act.

- Do you avoid talking, making eye contact or other interactions with the child while Time-Out is in effect?

- Do you make sure the child meets the requirements (quiet and in the seat) before releasing him or her from Time-Out?

- Do you place the child in Time-Out *every* time you should?

- Do you make sure the child either (a) complies with your original command or (b) completes a follow-up instruction after being released?

- Do you provide lots of positive attention when the child does complete the Time-Out?

- Is everyone following the same rules and procedures for Time-Out?

Warnings

Once your child understands how Time-Out works and cooperates with the procedure, you may wish to begin to use a single warning in some situations. There are times when circumstances keep you from being able to deliver a Time-Out immediately. For example, suppose you are in a rush to get to an appointment or school and your daughter will not put on her shoes. If you give the instruction and she does not comply, decide quickly whether you have the time, energy or other resources to follow through completely with discipline. If not, just do what you need to do to get the child out the door and deliver a Time-Out at the next convenient time, reminding her of the earlier infraction.

When the child gets home from school say something like, "You did not get your shoes on this morning when I asked so you have Time-Out before you play." This is not as good as delivering a Time-Out right away, but it is better than nothing.

If you decide you do have the resources and the commitment to follow through right away, deliver a single warning that always takes this form: "I said to put on your shoes or go to Time-Out." Giving this warning is like turning on a big, red flashing light that says to your child: I AM SERIOUS! Do not give a warning like this unless you are 100 percent committed to following through to the end with discipline. You should not expect the warning to have any effect if you have not built up your credibility with the child by following through with lots of previous disciplinary interactions.

JOB CARD GROUNDING

What Time-Out is for younger children, Job Card Grounding is for older children (about age eight and older) and adolescents. Like Time-Out, this approach includes suspension of *all* privileges for a brief time, then requires the child to earn them back by doing something appropriate, helpful or constructive. The time without privileges is longer (usually somewhere between fifteen and thirty minutes for an elementary school-aged child and four to twenty-four hours for an adolescent), but, like Time-Out, the same length of time is used no matter what the problem behavior was. Instead of giving the child an instruction to follow to earn back privileges, the child is assigned a predetermined task written on an index card.

The punishment in Job Card Grounding is the loss of privileges. The extra jobs themselves should not be considered a punishment, but instead an opportunity for the child to earn back privileges. Parents are sometimes tempted to quickly add more time or more jobs when the child does not comply right away, but this is not likely to significantly improve the effectiveness of Job Card Grounding and should be done with caution. In fact, some children will try to bait their parents into over reacting so they can accuse them of breaking the rules for Job Card Grounding. Focus on being consistent and making sure the child is truly grounded from all privileges.

Preparation

1. **Be sure expectations for the child are appropriate and have been communicated clearly.**

2. **Determine how long the child is to be grounded when expectations are not met.**

    - For grade school children, somewhere between fifteen minutes and an hour or two is appropriate.

    - For middle school students, two to four hours and for high school students, four to twenty-four hours.

    - The key is to identify a length of time that the child will find inconvenient and "painful," but not so lengthy that it seems pointless or too difficult to try to meet the requirements.

    - The idea is to encourage the child to get back on track by completing the necessary steps, not just to punish them or make them discouraged.

3. **Develop a list of fifteen or twenty or more jobs that need to be done regularly in your home (see the suggested list on the following page).**

    - The term *jobs* is used to distinguish the tasks from regularly assigned chores.

    - Jobs on the list should include the following features:

        – Not part of the child's regular chores

        – Will take around fifteen to thirty minutes to complete correctly

        – Currently being done by parents or someone else in the household (or not at all)

        – Within the child's ability level?

4. **Write a description of each job on a separate index card.**

    - The description should include enough detail to make it clear to everyone how the job is to be completed. Something like this:

Vacuum the Car

1. Empty all papers from the ashtray.

2. Wipe dashboard and ashtray with a damp paper towel.

3. Remove any trash from the floor or under the seats.

4. Use portable vacuum to vacuum all carpet, seats, rear deck, and all upholstered surfaces on the doors.

5. Return portable vacuum to the hall closet.

6. Throw used paper towels in trash.

5. Identify a "discussion time," a specific daily or weekly time when you will be available for the child to talk to about any issue (including complaints about Job Cards) without fear of earning additional consequences. Make sure you are available at the scheduled time.

6. Choose a time and explain the Job Card Grounding program to the child.

Procedure

1. **When a rule is broken or when chores or other assigned tasks not completed on time or in an acceptable way, the child is immediately grounded from *all* privileges for the length of time you have decided and assigned a Job Card.**

    -   The child picks the Job Card at random from among those the parent has prepared.

    -   Fan the cards out face down and tell the child he or she has earned a Job Card and must pick one. If the child chooses not to pick the Job Card, the parent selects *two* cards at random.

    -   If the child argues or complains when assigned a Job Card, additional Job Cards may be assigned for arguing or complaining (see Troubleshooting later in this section).

2. **Being grounded means**

    -   Attending school

    -   Completing regular chores

    -   Following household rules

    -   Losing *all* privileges, including (but not limited to)

        a. Television, DVD player
        b. Telephone and cell phone
        c. Radio, MP3 player, CD player, etc.
        d. Computer
        e. Games and toys (including video games)
        f. Playing outside
        g. Use of car, bicycle, skateboard, scooter or other vehicle

h. Visiting friends or having friends over

i. Snacks

j. Social activities of any kind, such as movies, going out to eat

k. Rewards or privileges earned earlier are not lost permanently, but suspended during the grounding. The child may not spend money or "cash in" other rewards during this time.

Be sure the child understands you are not taking back what they have already earned.

During the grounding, allowable activities include

- Eating meals (but not snacks)

- Sleeping
  (at approved times, not during the grounding)

- Working on chores or Job Cards

- Attending school or church

Otherwise, the child is to sit at the kitchen or dining room table and read or do homework.

- If this is inconvenient for the rest of the family, the child may spend the time in his or her room or other assigned area instead, but *only* if the room does not contain any of the privileges named previously.

3. **Usually, it is best not to take away privileges you cannot give back.**

- Even when grounded, the child should be allowed to participate in team sports (but no socializing before or after the game) and life events like recitals, prom or homecoming.

- If misbehavior is severe or persistent, consideration may be given to withholding even these privileges.

4. **Make sure you ground the child only from things you are sure you can control.**

   - You will only look ineffective if the child can sneak or "bootleg" something you have supposedly grounded them from when you are not looking.

   - Better to include fewer items and restrict access reliably.

5. **You may need to plan to have a babysitter or other adult supervision available if the child is grounded and unable to accompany you on an errand or family outing.**

   - If you must leave and babysitting cannot be arranged, the child must accompany you and the grounding begins or continues when you return.

6. **During the grounding, parents must observe the following rules:**

   - Action, not talk

     a. No nagging, lecturing, or arguing

     b. No reminders about the need to complete the Job Cards

     c. No discussion of the grounding

     d. No explanations of the rules

     e. No reminders of previous behavior problems

7. **Grounding continues until *all three* of the following conditions have been met:**

    *   The minimum grounding time you assigned has passed with the child having no privileges

    *   The child has corrected whatever earned the grounding if it can be corrected

    *   The assigned Job Card has been completed acceptably

    The child may choose when to correct the problem and when to complete the Job Card, but does not earn privileges back until this has been done. Grounding may last for only the minimum time or for several days or more if the child chooses not to complete the requirements more promptly.

    Parents are not to remind the child that there are Job Cards to be completed or add further consequences if the child chooses not to complete the Job Card promptly.

8. **When the child has corrected the problem (if it is correctable) and completed the Job Card, a parent must check to be sure the job is done correctly.**

    *   If the job is performed correctly, the child should be praised for accepting consequences and completing the job appropriately and informed of when privileges will be restored.

    *   If the Job is not completed correctly, a parent should review the description of the job with the child and provide feedback on what parts were done correctly and what parts need improvement and (without nagging or complaining) instruct the child to redo the incorrect portions of the task.

- If the job is not completed correctly on the second attempt, no further attempts are allowed for one hour.

Delivering Job Cards

When a rule is broken, implement Job Card Grounding as soon as possible. Work to maintain a calm, matter-of fact approach to delivering Job Cards. Follow these steps:

1. **Identify the problem:**

   - Focus on specific behaviors ("You did not let me know where you were after school today.").

   - Focus on the present situation only, do not bring up past difficulties.

   - Do not talk about motives (do not ask why the youth broke the rule).

2. **Deliver the consequence:**

   - Tell the child he or she is grounded and has earned a Job Card.

3. **Establish the alternative behavior:**

   - "You need to let me know where you are after school."

   - Refer to the list of rules if possible.

4. **Add an earn back requirement:**

   - Have the child select a Job Card or pick two for them.

   - Identify what needs to be fixed, if possible (homework finished, chore completed).

Summary

1. The child breaks a rule or fails to complete a chore by the expected time or to the expected standard.

2. The child is immediately grounded from all privileges and is assigned a Job Card.

3. The child is eligible to earn back privileges after a minimum time, but grounding ends only when the child has corrected whatever led to the grounding and completed the Job Card in an acceptable way.

Troubleshooting

1. If the child responds to getting a Job Card with further inappropriate behaviors, such as arguing or complaining, do the following:

   - Deliver a calm warning in this form: "You are starting to argue. You may stop now, or you will get another Job Card."

     a. If the child has not stopped the unacceptable behavior within thirty seconds, deliver an additional Job Card (but don't extend the grounding) and walk away.

     b. Be sure you are not being drawn into discussions, explanations or arguments.

     c. If the child continues to complain about too much work, unfairness or similar complaints, say something like, "I can understand how you would feel that way," and walk away.

2. If the grounding seems to be lasting an excessively long time:

   - Be sure the child's life is sufficiently interesting or rewarding when not grounded.

   - Add a daily allowance for days when no Job Cards are earned.

   - Make weekend privileges contingent on staying under a target number of groundings during the week.

   - Check to be sure that your child's life is dull enough during the grounding.

   - Check to be sure your child is not "bootlegging" restricted items when you are not around.

   - Be sure you are not providing attention in the form of nagging, reminders, discussions or emotional reactions during the grounding.

Suggestions for Job Card Jobs

Sweep/Mop

laundry room floor

basement

garage

kitchen floor

patio

sidewalks

entryway

driveway

Vacuum

living room

dining room

family room

steps

bedroom(s)

hallway(s)

basement

car(s)

Scrub

kitchen floor

basement floor

bathroom floor(s)

laundry room floor

toilet(s)

sink(s)

garbage cans

kitty litter box

aquarium/fish bowl

bird cage

hamster/gerbil cage

Clean

patio glass doors

shower door(s)

windows

mirrors

car windows

refrigerator interior

deck/patio furniture

oven

fireplace

Dust

living room

family room

dining room

ceiling fan(s)

bedroom(s)

basement

Wash/Wipe

kitchen cupboards (inside) kitchen cupboards (outside)

basement walls

baseboard

microwave (inside and out)

refrigerator exterior

door and window frames

dishes

pots and pans

stove exterior

shutters

light fixtures

Pick up/Organize

shelves in garage

shelves in laundry room "junk" drawer

hall closet

bedroom closet

dresser drawers

toy box

Laundry

sort dirty laundry

fold towels

put towels away

sort & put away a load

change linens on bed(s)

wash and dry all bedding

ironing

Miscellaneous

"pooper scoop" yard

wash car(s)

wash dog(s)

rake leaves

hose off driveway/patio

polish door knobs

pull weeds

water all plants

clean shed

load/unload dishwasher

do a sibling's chore

shake out rugs

EIGHT

Some Specific Strategies for Some Specific Problems

B ack in my teaching days at the medical school, the students had a saying: If you hear hoof beats, think horses, not zebras. What this means is that we should think of the most likely or common cause for something first, not the rarest or most exotic. In other words, common events happen often, uncommon events happen rarely.

One of the things that keeps the practice of psychology interesting (and challenging) is the seemingly endless list of difficult situations people bring to my office. Just when I think I have heard it all, someone will come up with a new and creative way to get into a bind. These situations may be interesting, but they are zebras, they don't come up all that often.

Most of my time is spent talking with kids and parents about more common issues, the "symptoms of life" mentioned earlier.

Just about every parent struggles with some of these issues at one time or another—things such as not listening, bedtime problems, acting out in public, and kids not picking up after themselves. Improvement with these behaviors almost always leads to more general improvement in behavior, even some you have not worked on directly.

So, here are targeted methods designed to respond to some of the most common problem behaviors. All of these techniques have been used numerous times with good success by parents of my clients. It is not possible to outline a response for every problem behavior, but the following examples should give you some specific direction on dealing with some of these issues and also give you a good sense of how to respond to similar issues in the future. Wherever possible, the guidelines are presented step-by-step or in an outline format to make them easier to refer back to quickly in the future.

Keep in mind that you are not likely to have much success with any strategy if you have not developed good basic compliance. If your child is not used to following your instructions or does not believe you will follow through with promised consequences, he or she is not likely to respond well to any other method. Your first and most important efforts should focus on making sure your children follow instructions reliably and take care of routine responsibilities in a routine way. If your children do not follow your instructions the first time you give them at least 60 or 70 percent of the time, you should invest some time training compliance until you reach this level.

PROBLEM: NOT LISTENING

Compliance Training Procedure

Before starting this training, be sure you are familiar with Time-In and Time-Out procedures. The goal of this training is to provide concentrated and successful practice with following instructions in a situation you control. Setting aside time for this allows you to get lots of practice in a short amount of time and helps both you and the child learn the procedures. Any time you find that your child (and you) are slipping back into old habits, you should consider doing compliance training again.

1. **Set aside fifteen to thirty minutes for Compliance Training.**

2. **Arrange a room to provide more opportunities for training and to support success.**

Set up numerous small tasks that can be enforced physically, hand-over-hand if necessary. This will assure the child eventually follows 100 percent of your instructions during the training and earns praise and positive attention for each appropriate behavior. This means they will get lots of practice in a short amount of time. For example:

- Put toys or other objects on the floor or out of place.

- Open drawers slightly.

- Move furniture slightly.

- Turn on lights, electronics or other objects the child knows how to turn off.

3. **Bring the child to the room and, after a short time, give an instruction using the Guidelines for Giving Effective Instructions.**

   • If the child follows the instruction, provide lots of praise and positive attention. Create a big effect to let them know you appreciate it when they listen. Wait a few seconds then give another command.

   • If the child does not comply, implement Time-Out following the guidelines explained earlier.

   • If the child does not comply the second time you give the instruction, repeat Time-Out.

   • After releasing the child from Time-Out the second time, take the child's hand in yours, then repeat the instruction while "helping them" to complete the task.

   • Provide praise and positive attention, wait a few seconds, then give another command and repeat the process

4. **Continue daily training (or more often if you are able) until your child is compliant with atleast 60 to 70 percent of commands the first time they are given.**

5. **Use this procedure to get back on track any time noncompliant or defiant behavior seems to be increasing.**

PROBLEM: STEALING

The first step in dealing with minor thefts is to make sure you know what belongs to your child. If you have been lax in allowing your child to borrow or lend toys, clothes or other items, this will be more difficult. Then, make sure your children understand the rules for possessions. Choose an appropriate time to inform them of the following rules:

1. **They are not allowed to have items that do not belong to them, regardless of whether they were found, borrowed or given to them.**

2. **If you find they have something that does not belong to them, you will return it or donate it and inform the person or store that you took it from.**

3. **You will then go into their room, find a possession of theirs with similar value and give it away or throw it away.**

4. **You will do this each and every time you find they have anything that does not belong to them.**

5. **If necessary, you will check pockets, book bag or any other place the child might keep things when they leave and when they come home.**

At this point, I usually suggest the parent tell the child something like, "If you find a $100 bill lying in the street, you might as well leave it there. Because if you bring it home and I find it, I will get rid of the $100 bill and $100 worth of your stuff." If they steal again, make sure to remove something of theirs they really care about. For most children, it takes only one or two times for them to get the message.

PROBLEM: CLOTHING, TOYS OR OTHER PERSONAL ITEMS LEFT OUT

Your first choice should be to tell the child to pick up and to enforce the instruction the way you usually would if they don't listen (Time-Out or something similar). If the problem has been going on for some time or continues to occur, consider one or both of the following.

Option 1:

1. When items are found left out where or when they should not be, rather than just complaining or nagging,), pick them up yourself. Your goal then becomes to remind the child that you are holding on to these items, but without having to tell them.

2. Put the items in a garbage bag or bin. Use something made out of clear plastic if you can so the child can actually see the items and be reminded they don't get to have them.

3. Put a piece of tape on the bag or bin and mark it with the date one or two weeks from that day, then put the bag in a place the child will see it often.

4. On the date written on the bag, remove the items and dump them out somewhere near where you found them in the first place.

5. Give the child a deadline for having them picked up. If the items are not picked up on time, repeat the process.

6. If the child does not pick them up after the second or third opportunity (you decide), the items are not wanted and should be disposed of. Don't make a big show of disposing of the items or even tell the child that you are

getting rid of the things. This will only give them a chance to say, "I don't care." Wait for a time when they are not around and dispose of the items. When they ask about the items, tell them casually that, because they chose not to pick them up, you assumed they did not want them and got rid of them. Do not lecture. Do not nag (not that you would ever, ever do that).

Option 2:

It's probably a good idea to do something like this even if you already have done Option 1. Begin by deciding what you think is a reasonable amount of space to devote to storage of your children's things and then take the following steps. You may be surprised at how much more your children value each of their toys if they don't have free access to them all the time.

1. Have the child help you organize toys in bins or other containers. They are allowed to keep only what can fit into the bins. Allow them to decide which items to keep or not, but don't compromise on the space.

2. Once the toys are organized, the child may "check out" one bin of toys at a time.

3. The first bin must be "checked in" (picked up and put away) before another can be checked out.

PROBLEM: BAD BEHAVIOR IN PUBLIC PLACES

Kids often learn that they can get away with more misbehavior in public places because parents don't have as much control over these environments. Department stores, restaurants (see below), church, and grocery stores are common settings for tantrums and other problem behaviors. Keep in mind that, unless you are shopping for toys or buying their favorite treats, these can be boring places to be for kids. Often, misbehavior is just a product of their efforts to make the situation more interesting, so finding more productive ways to make it more enjoyable for them should be part of your thinking.

If your child consistently acts out in these kinds of places, you should probably go back to compliance training for a time. Public places are not the best place to try to teach kids to follow instructions, but more of an indicator of how things are going. You will do better to work on following instructions under circumstances you choose, like at home. Otherwise, consider the following recommendations.

1. **Make sure children are rested, fed and have used the bathroom before you go out. Physically uncomfortable kids are likely to make you uncomfortable too.**

2. **If necessary, practice making brief "trial runs" to the store or other public places. Go to the grocery to buy just a gallon of milk. Your child has a better chance of succeeding (and being rewarded) on a shorter trip.**

3. **Let the child know about how long you expect to be there or what you plan to buy and what you don't.**

4. **Tell the child how you expect him or her to act: remind the child of the rules in the car or immediately before entering. Keep it simple, something like:**

   - They are to stay within arm's reach

   - They are to ask permission before touching anything

- You will allow them to pick a treat at check out if they have behaved well. They will lose this privilege if they ask before the checkout line.

5. **Keep them involved and let them help (for example, talk about what you are buying, have them get items from the shelf).**

6. **Consider allowing them to bring some quiet diversion (such as a small toy or book) to keep them occupied.**

7. **Praise and touch often when they are following the rules.**

8. **Use Time-Out on the floor, shopping cart, bathroom or car if needed.**

9. **Decide whether it is appropriate to leave.**

- If you believe the child wants to leave, require them to stay until they are behaving appropriately, otherwise you will encourage them to act up whenever they want to leave somewhere.

- If you believe the child wants to stay, leave. Then restrict privileges at home for at least as much time as you would have spent at the store.

PROBLEM: ACTING OUT WHILE DINING OUT

I probably shouldn't be, but I continue to be surprised at the extent of bad behavior by children in restaurants. Kids wander around as if they were in their living room, dragging a toy or blanket around behind them, inspecting other people's meals, talking and making noise. Meanwhile, their parents seem to be intent on finishing their own meals without being bothered by having to discipline their kids. Of course, I am not the only one who sees this. Your kids see other children doing this too and may think it is okay for them to behave this way also.

As always, you should be sure your child has been informed of your expectations. Reminding children of the rules (and consequences) before you get out of the car or right before you walk into the restaurant is a good idea. Even before that, try to make sure your child is feeling all right, has used the bathroom and is well rested before you go. Tired, unhappy children tend not to make good dinner companions. Once you get inside, do the following:

1. **Find the best seat (isolated, against a wall, a booth if possible), away from distractions.**

2. **Keep the child within reach.**

3. **Bring crackers or ask the wait staff for crackers.**

4. **Allow child to order something he or she will enjoy.**

5. **Bring interesting toys or other activities (small, quiet, independent).**

6. **Take the toys away when the food comes.**

7. **Use Time-Out in a bathroom, car or other suitable place as needed.**

8. **Restrict privileges at home for about the amount of time you had to deal with their behavior at the restaurant.**

PROBLEM: STALLING OR REFUSING BEDTIME

Like some other situations we have talked about in this section, going to bed can sometimes seem like being punished. If the child is doing something enjoyable and has to stop to get ready for bed, they are being asked to go from an interesting situation to a boring one.

This is one reason we always suggest having a good bedtime routine (explained next) that emphasizes slowing down and getting ready for sleep. This eases the transition to quiet time and sleep, instead of asking the child to move abruptly from a high-interest, high-energy activity to lying quietly in bed. I meet a lot of parents who are frustrated with the other parent for getting the kids wound up at bedtime by wrestling with them or doing some other stimulating activity. This is one situation where we want to reduce contrast, not increase it.

Sleeping is another one of those things you can't make your kid do and they know it. So if they are inclined to be defiant, this is a time you are likely to see the defiance flare up. Success at bedtime requires (1) a good sleep environment, (2) good bedtime routines, and (3) a motivated sleeper. The following guidelines should help in most cases:

Preparation

- Make sure you have good instructional control during the day (do compliance training, if needed).

- Do not use the bedroom as your main place discipline. If your child is often upset or agitated when they go into their room, they will come to associate the room with being upset instead of thinking of it as a place to be relaxed and calm.

- The room should be comfortably cool, quiet, and dark (a night light is okay, but brighter lights and TV interfere with good sleep).

- The bed should be comfortable and not be filled with toys or other things that may cause discomfort and wake the child during the night.

- Keep a consistent wake time. Even on weekends, the child should get up within an hour or so of their school day wake time. If the child continues to have difficulty getting to sleep, setting an earlier wake time is often a good first step.

- Focus on getting the child stay in the bedroom and be quiet, not trying to get to sleep on command (you cannot "make them" go to sleep anyway).

Set a bedtime:

1. **Start by keeping track of when your child falls asleep most nights. Putting your child to bed before they are prepared for sleep will probably make the situation worse, not better. They will have trouble settling and get used to being awake and active in their room at night.**

2. **Set this as the temporary bedtime.**

3. Gradually move the bedtime earlier over several weeks as the child adjusts.

Set up a consistent night-time routine:

1. Do the same procedures in the same order at the same time each night.

2. Focus on calm and enjoyable activities within an hour or so of bedtime (bath, story).

3. Avoid stimulating, energetic activities (video games, outside play, wrestling).

4. If necessary, make a list or chart showing the steps.

Follow a regular bedtime routine

1. Tell the child it is time for bed.

2. Escort the child to the bedroom, tuck them in, say prayers or read a book if this is part of the routine, say "goodnight" and walk out.

   • Ignore complaints or protests.

   • If the child complains too much during this time, walk out.

3. If the child stays in the room and quiet, do nothing, even if he or she is moving around

4. If the child cries or yells, but stays in the room, remind them once that it is bedtime,

   • If crying and yelling continues, check on the child after a few minutes.

   • Continue to check in every few minutes as long as crying and yelling continues.

- The purpose of these visits is to reassure the child you are still there.

- Keep the visits at a minute or less.

- Do not lie down with the child.

- Do not attempt to soothe or comfort or get into a discussion.

- Repeat calmly, "It is bedtime now," and leave.

5. **If the child leaves the bedroom,**

   - Return the child to the bedroom using the least physical guidance necessary.

   - Tell the child if he or she leaves the room again, you will close the door.

   - If the child leaves the room again, put him or her back in bed and close the door for a minute or two (do not lock the child in the bedroom).

   - Open the door:

     a. If the child is in bed or at least settled and quiet, provide praise and leave the door open.

     b. If the child is out of bed, return them to bed and close the door for a little longer time.

     c. Add a minute or two each time you have to close the door.

6. **Reward success the next morning. Focus on what was accomplished (even small things), not what went wrong.**

7. **Stay consistent and be persistent. This sometimes can take several weeks.**

PROBLEM: LYING

Kids lie. Some kids lie a lot. Many parents seem to find this behavior particularly disturbing, maybe because of the moral aspect of not telling the truth or just because it seems like a big sign of disrespect. But, like every other behavior, if your kids see you react emotionally to lying, they will realize that it can be a powerful tool for them to use to manage your behavior. Lying is an annoying behavior, but it's just a behavior. Don't make it more than it is. Focus on the behavior that led them to be dishonest, not on the lying itself.

Think about this from your children's point of view. If you ask them about something they did wrong and they tell you the truth, there is a 100 percent chance they will get whacked. If they lie, there is at least some chance they can get away with it. From their perspective, setting aside the morality, lying is a better choice. When there is a threat of a harsh or unreasonable punishment, there is even more incentive for them to be dishonest.

Some kids tip off the fact they are lying; some are much better at it. The most reliable indicator for most children seems to be what they do with their eyes. If they look away when you are talking, this is a good sign they are being less than truthful. They also may shuffle their feet or shift from one foot to the other. There is no certain way to know whether a child is lying, but many children give signals of this kind.

Try to avoid talking too much about lying. Don't accuse. Instead, focus on a positive value by telling them you are asking them to be honest with you. Above all, make sure you recognize and reward honesty any time it does occur.

- If you *think* the child is lying, the child is lying.

- If you already know the truth, do not demand the truth from the child:

  - From the child's perspective, they have a better chance of getting a consequence if they tell the truth.

  - Let them know what you know about the situation from the beginning. You are a parent, not a police interrogator.

  - Demanding a "confession" often encourages more lies.

- Respond as you would to any inappropriate behavior (Time-Out, grounding).

- Do not lecture about morality at this time.

- If the lie is about an unintentional behavior (like spilling the juice), make it clear that the consequence is for the lie, not the accident.

Some children do have a more serious problem with lying. It seems they will not tell the truth about anything. They lie about even the most unimportant things. If you have followed these guidelines for a time and the situation still does not improve, it is probably best to seek professional help.

PROBLEM: MISSED CURFEW OR OTHER DEADLINE

For most older children, being with friends is more fun than being at home. This means that coming home is a little like getting a Time-Out. They are being asked to go from a more fun and interesting situation to a less enjoyable one. There is contrast here, but it is in the wrong direction. The fact that they drag their feet a little is not too surprising, but that does not mean you shouldn't respond.

The problem of missed curfews often develops over time because parents have been "flexible" with deadlines. If the child can get away with being ten minutes late, he or she will likely try fifteen, then twenty and so on. They will probably continue to push until you push back. Their excuses may sound reasonable, and you may be convinced to cut them some slack. Resist this temptation except in extraordinary circumstances. Remember, the last one on the plane gets to go, but the next one doesn't. Too late is too late. Take the following steps:

1. **Set an alarm clock for the curfew time. This is the only time that matters. Not the clock in their friend's car or their cell phone. Only your clock counts. Use the clock near your bed if you do not want to wait up for them. This will also allow you to check on their condition when they come home.**

2. **The child is responsible for turning off the alarm.**

If the alarm does not go off, they are on time, even if they turn it off one second before it would sound. Enjoy your good night of sleep and recognize and reward their on-time behavior the next day. If the alarm goes off, they are late and earn a consequence. I usually recommend

- One to fifteen minutes late loses an hour off curfew the next weekend night.

- More than fifteen minutes late earns staying home the next weekend night.

You also can use this method for other deadlines such as turning off electronics or coming to the kitchen for meals or bedtime.

PROBLEM: LIMITED DIET OR FOOD REFUSAL

About nine times out of ten, if a parent describes their child as a picky eater, I know without being told what foods the child will eat: pizza, chicken nuggets, french fries, chips and so on. These are the foods most kids will choose to eat if they are allowed to.

I once had a client who ate nothing but one particular brand of frozen french fries for more than a year because his parents were afraid he would starve himself if they did not feed his habit. Once he was allowed to miss a couple of "meals," he regained his appetite for other foods.

Going to bed without supper used to be considered a reasonable response to misbehavior. I don't recommend this as a regular approach, but I do know that hunger tends to broaden one's idea of what is an acceptable food. Even a willful child tends to get a little more cooperative when their stomach starts growling. Here are things to consider if your child is one of those picky eaters:

1. **Maintain mealtime schedules and routines. Keep your mealtimes as regular as possible so your children are actually hungry when they sit down to eat.**

   - Eat too often and they will still be working on digesting the last meal.

- Eat too seldom or too inconsistently, and they will probably be snacking or grazing often.

2. **Control access to food and snack items between meals. Better still, limit the snacks you have available at all. They can't eat what you don't have. If you do have snacks around, keep track of them.**

    - Do not allow food or beverages (other than water) within one hour of meal time.

3. **Offer only two menu choices for every meal: (1) Take it, or (2) Leave it.**

    - Do not prepare an alternative meal (peanut butter sandwiches seem particularly popular for this purpose).

4. **Provide reasonable portions of all foods, but do not allow access to preferred foods until after the child has eaten the non-preferred items.** (*First the Broccoli, Then the Ice Cream*).

5. **If the child continually complains about a particular main course item, do not set a place for them the next time you serve that item. When they ask where their plate is, just tell them that you know they do not like that food so you assumed they would want to skip this meal.**

6. **If a child leaves the table, dawdles excessively, or acts up, allow them to be excused from the table and do the following:**

    - Do not allow anything fun or interesting until the rest of the family has finished their meal

    - Ignore the uncooperative child during this time. Do not allow him or her to return to the table. If the child does come back, tell them they have been excused.

- Give lots of extra praise, positive attention, or privileges to those still seated at the table.

- Do not allow the child to eat anything or drink anything other than water until the next meal time.

7. **The next time the child does participate in a meal, do not mention the previous difficulties.**

8. **Make snacks available only to children who ate the last meal completely.**

The overwhelming majority of children will decide to eat just about anything you put in front of them after missing a meal or two. Some children do have more profound difficulty with eating, however. *If total food refusal persists for three days or more, consult a pediatrician or behavioral psychologist.*

WHEN ICE CREAM IS NOT ENOUGH

Most normal children behave in ways that are inappropriate and sometimes in ways that are disturbing, though they may not think of their own behavior in this way. It takes an adult to help them recognize where they are going wrong and train them away from these actions and toward more constructive behavior. That is really what this book is about in its essence: reducing or eliminating unacceptable or disturbing behavior and training productive behavior.

Most often, making constructive changes in household disciplinary and motivational systems along with a little more intensive effort on the part of parents will help children behave better and develop an improved outlook on life, or at least get them moving in that direction.

Sometimes, though, these changes are not enough. Some children have more serious problems with behavior, mood or adjustment. They do not respond well, or at least do not respond fully to the approach that works for most issues with most children. Often, as we have discussed before, these more serious concerns are not entirely clear until we have worked on the basic issues of compliance and motivation. We can't tell what the "can't do" issues are until we deal with the "won't do."

More serious problems can develop in a number of ways.

- Some children have biologically based problems or have inherited traits that make them more vulnerable to life's stresses. Many times, I see children whose struggles remind their parents of their own difficult childhoods.

- Some children experience difficult circumstances early in life when they were denied adequate stimulation or affection. At times, their parents have been so consumed with dealing with their own issues that they have great difficulty meeting the challenges of parenting, no matter how hard they try.

- Some children have been moved from place to place within a family or the human services system and have never developed a solid sense of place or security.

- For others, the problems emerge after they have experienced a traumatic event of some kind.

Any of these circumstances, and others, can make it difficult for these children to respond to the world in a productive way. Sometimes it is extremely difficult to determine why a child continues to struggle emotionally and behaviorally.

I tend to trust parents. The majority of the time, if the parent (or grandparent, foster parent or other caregiver) who spends the most time with the child believes there is a more significant problem, it is usually worth looking into. If your child, or any child you know, has problems that seem very severe or persistent, you should consider contacting a pediatrician or family physician or, better still, a psychologist who has experience working with children and families, particularly someone who specializes in behavioral pediatrics.

There is no way for me to list every behavior that should be cause for concern, but the following items would definitely be included:

- If the child seems to be chronically sad, unhappy or irritable.

- If there is a sudden and significant change in eating or sleeping habits that cannot be accounted for by ordinary circumstances.

- If the child has trouble coping with requirements of day-to-day life, seems to be overwhelmed by stress over ordinary events, or expresses intense fear about common events or situations.

- If there is a sudden significant drop in performance in academics or other area.

- It the child develops odd or unusual habits, such as intense interest in cleaning, organizing or other repetitive actions.

- If the child is excessively aggressive or cruel to pets or siblings.

- If the child engages in dangerous or self-injurious behavior, shows physical signs of having caused intentional self-harm, or indicates a loss of interest in life or a desire to harm or kill himself or herself.

- If the child withdraws from family activities, friends, or things he or she used to enjoy

- If teachers or other people who know your child well suggest you may want to consider seeking help.

- If the child seems incapable of responding to the basic parenting skills you have learned.

Please keep in mind that no book, website, radio program, or list of signs and symptoms can substitute for individual consultation with a trained mental health professional or qualified physician. If you are in doubt about whether you should seek professional help for mental or behavioral health issues, contact the child's primary care physician for advice. If a more serious problem does exist, the sooner you get assistance, the better your chances for a good outcome for your child.

NINE

The ABCs
of Deliberate Discipline

T he purpose of this final section is to provide a summary of much of what we have discussed in previous chapters, but also to serve as a quick way for you to review or remind yourself of some of these ideas and methods in the future. You may forget many of the details over time, but if you remember the main concepts and goals, there is a good chance you can make the necessary adjustments in your methods as your children grow and mature. Trust yourself, trust your children and follow these general guidelines, and your prospects for success are good.

Acceptance

- Accept the child unconditionally, but *do not* accept the child's behavior unconditionally.

- Accept that children have free will and may choose to behave differently than you would like, give them room to both succeed and fail.

- Accept and exercise the role, authority and responsibility of parenthood.

Accountability

- Establish clear, firm, specific and developmentally appropriate expectations and hold the child to them.

- Deliver consequences, not lectures.

Attention

- Pay attention to what you pay attention to:

    - Recognize and respond to acceptable (not just exceptional) behavior.

    - Do not overreact to typical child behavior.

    - Do not be drawn into emotionally charged disciplinary interactions with your child.

- Pay attention or pay the price:

    - Monitor whereabouts, associations, and activities.

    - Trust, but check.

Action

- Develop a planned, structured approach to dealing with behavior and use it consistently.

- Respond to behavior, don't just talk about it, don't just hope it will change.

- Talk less, act more when delivering discipline.

Behave Like an Adult

- Continue to develop your own interests and relationships.

- Be patient; recognize that behavior changes gradually (remember the potter's wheel example).

- Deal with today's behavior today.

- Be friendly, but don't try to be a friend.

- Respect and support the authority of other adults.

- Be the person you want your child to be; model the behavior you expect from them.

- Jump ahead, don't jump in (let natural consequences happen).

- Protect, but don't pamper.

- Respond to misbehavior reliably, but without excessive emotion or discussion (just like gravity).

C

Communication

- Use age appropriate content, methods and timing to make sure your message is heard:

  - Give clear, effective instructions.

  - Write down expectations when appropriate (which is most of the time).

- Tell the child what you want, not just what you don't want.

- Explaining something the first time is information, the second time is nagging.

- Be willing to listen (but not necessarily agree with) the child's point of view.

Contingency

- *First the Broccoli, Then the Ice Cream:*

  - Make privileges available only when expectations are met.

- Respond according to the child's behavior:

  - If you see a behavior you like, pay attention to it and reward or reinforce it.

  - If you see a behavior you don't like, ignore or punish it.

  - Repeat.

Contrast

- Respond reliably to both appropriate and inappropriate behavior:

- Reinforce behaviors you want more of, make it more interesting for the child to do things you like.

- Ignore or punish behaviors you want less of.

Consistency

- Assure that the same behaviors always lead to the same consequences.

- Assure that all adults in the child's life respond to behavior in a similar way.

- Develop a plan and follow it ... and follow it ... and follow it ... and follow it.

About the Author

I f life experience can help a therapist better understand his clients, Tim Riley should be well equipped for the job. Before earning his doctorate in psychology, Dr. Riley worked selling toys in a department store, as a carpenter, delivery driver, farmhand, clown, warehouse worker and forklift driver, graphic artist, editor, and owner/operator of a screen printing business.

Along the way, he found time to marry and help rear three children (Nicole, Kara and Andrew), coaching baseball, softball, basketball, and volleyball, and cheering on everything else. He is a surprisingly unskilled amateur musician, woodworker, and juggler who subscribes to the idea that aging is inevitable, but maturity is not. Dr. Riley and his wife, Debra, make their home in Elkhorn, a small community on the western edge of Omaha, Nebraska.

Before moving to his current full-time private practice, Dr. Riley spent several years as an Assistant Professor of Pediatrics at the University of Nebraska Medical Center. During his time at UNMC, he directed the Attention Deficit and Related Disorders Diagnostic Clinic and the Outreach Behavioral Health Clinics program. In addition, he acted as the team psychologist for traveling specialty clinics for Genetics and Medically Handicapped Children, working closely with physicians and other medical and educational professionals in communities across the state.

Dr. Riley also has served on the faculties of the University of Nebraska and Bellevue University. He has made numerous presentations and conducted workshops for parents, mental health and medical professionals, educators, and child care workers.

Dr. Riley is currently part of a group of twelve psychologists in a building shared with a pediatric medical clinic. His practice emphasizes work with children, adolescents, and families on a range of behavioral, emotional, and adjustment problems with special emphases on anxiety, stress and pain management, mood disorders, and ADD/ADHD.

Index